Recruitment in the 90s

Peter Herriot is a Fellow of the British Psychological Society and Professor of Occupational Psychology at Birkbeck College, University of London, a position he has held since 1981. He is a regular contributor to journals and periodicals on the topics of assessment in general, and graduate recruitment in particular. His most recent book is *Down from the Ivory Tower: Graduates and their Jobs* (1984), and he is currently editing a *Handbook of Assessment in Organisations,* to be published by Wiley in 1989.

Peter Herriot has done research and consultancy for a variety of public- and private-sector organizations, including the Ministry of Defence (Navy), Price Waterhouse, Trust House Forte and J. Sainsbury, on the design of recruitment procedures and on specific techniques. He is a regular speaker at the IPM Conference at Harrogate and spoke in 1988 on 'Assessment Centres: Fashionable Fad or Flexible Friend?'

Recruitment in the 90s

Peter Herriot

Institute of Personnel Management

First published 1989

© Peter Herriot 1989

Typeset by Action Typesetting, Gloucester
and printed in Great Britain by
Dotesios Printers Ltd., Trowbridge, Wiltshire

British Library Cataloguing Publication Data

Herriot, Peter
    Recruitment in the '90's
    1. Management
    I. Title II. Institute of Personnel Management
    658.3'11

    ISBN 0 – 85292 – 420-8

Contents

Chapter 1

What's So New About the 90s?

Trends

In one of my bedroom drawers there lives a large collection of extremely flowery kipper ties. I never wear them. Their sole purpose is to remind me (and hint to my children) that the 60s was my decade. We all have our personal decades, and we also have our national ones. The 40s were a decade of supreme struggle and post-war reconstruction. The 90s will be remembered by many organizations as their decade; many others won't be remembering it at all, since they will have ceased to exist. My contention in this book is that the events of the 90s will create such demands for change upon organizations that many will go under. And the major reason they will do so is that they will fail to recruit and retain the people they need to help them change. People make the place, and people set the pace.

We already know, or we can confidently guess, quite a few of these crucial trends and events. We know about the Single European Market, with its increased opportunities but, by the same token, increased competition; its implications for the necessary improvement in quality of goods and services are beginning to dawn upon us. One of the myths of the past decade has been that slimmer organizations produce better quality goods and services. Shedding of staff and increased productivity per employee have kept the City, the shareholders and the Chancellor happy. But what have they done for quality? Are goods any better designed or produced? Are services any more effective in meeting clients' wants and needs? Or are there the same numbers of Friday afternoon cars, dangerously designed domestic appliances, inedible meals, perilously overcrowded journeys, and delayed medical operations? Many public and private sector organizations have already been cut back. Competitive advantage can now only come from improved quality. The power of the accountant may be on the wane. Welcome back research and development, and design. Power to the customer and to the client. So the first emphasis will be on *quality*.

The second trend in the 90s will be the increasing impact of *information technology*. Some organizations have already changed their structures and managerial systems. Having engaged in extensive capital expenditure to automate production or services, they redesigned shopfloor jobs. Now they are redesigning managerial work. Information technology offers flexible decision support systems to all managers, so the distinction between technical and general managers is out of date. Many more organizations are just starting to think about these changes, and their implications for recruitment and training. They are also beginning to realize that, whether they like it or not, the decentralized provision of on-line information and decision systems means that power is redistributed down through the organization. The IT revolution gives both the shopfloor technician and the manager more information, more power and more responsibility. It requires a different structure and different people. Above all, it requires an understanding of how information technology is being used, and how these uses fit in with the organization's strategic policy. Some organizations are further along this road than others. What's for sure is that those who haven't integrated information technology by the end of the 90s will be dead. In the meantime, the survivors will be getting to grips with the next revolution — the biological one.

The third trend of the 90s is likely to be the ever-increasing *birth-rate and death-rate of organizations*. For each hi-tech science-park entrepreneur who succeeds in attracting start-up capital, there is another who is bought out. Acquisition of profitable new enterprises by medium-sized firms enables them to get into the big league. Once there, mergers and takeovers result in horrible clashes of incompatible cultures following forced marriages. Before these new bedfellows have a chance to get used to each other's annoying little habits, their monstrous and unmanageable size forces them to diversify and spawn new national or product divisions.

As if this internal chaos isn't enough, organizations have to pay more attention to their external environment — political, financial, technological, scientific. This is not just because these factors are complex and unpredictable, and changing ever more rapidly. It is also because the environment is more knowable. It is possible to learn instantly what the money markets of the world are doing. We know far more about the Soviet Union and China than we did ten years ago. Research teams in different countries race to beat their rivals. Because the environment is knowable, organizations cannot afford not to know it. Their competitors will, and so will many of their customers and clients. So the survival of organizations will depend more and more on their knowledge of the world. The fourth trend of the 90s, then, is the increasing importance of the *knowledge base*.

The final trend will be a change internal to organizations themselves. The *structure of organizations* will change so that the most common structure ceases to be the bureaucracy. All organizations have to live on the tight-rope of survival; but they have to look both sides to keep their balance. They have to ensure some degree of coordination and continuity within the organization in order to prevent disintegration. But they also have to look to the other side of the rope, to their environment. They have to adapt to or work upon their environment so as to survive within it. Bureaucracies are fine when the environment is nice and predictable, and you can meet its needs by the same products or services year in year out. They are dinosaurs when their environment requires them to change rapidly.

Much recent management theorizing has merely tinkered with bureaucracy. Matrix designs try to bridge the functional, product or national gaps. Subsidiaries have been split off from the parent organization, but such tight financial control has been kept by Big Daddy that they become mini-bureaucracies themselves. In the 90s, organizations will be forced to free up their structures. They will gradually be replaced by what Alvin Toffler called 'adhocracies', with project teams forming and disbanding when the job is done. Many of these employees will be temporary, on a fixed contract for the project, rather than permanent staff. The latter group, the organizational core, will be expected to change jobs repeatedly during their organizational career. They will have to perform the painful contortion of moving upwards and sideways at the same time.

So we have five major 90s trends:

- Increased competition and therefore a need for better quality goods and services
- Increased use of information technology, with consequences for the nature of managerial work and the decentralization of decision-making
- An increasing number of acquisitions, mergers, take-overs, and diversification
- An increase in the availability and quantity of knowledge about the environment
- A change in the structure of organizations such that bureaucracies give way to 'adhocracies'.

Responses

All of these trends imply the need for organizations to think and plan strategically. Such plans will undoubtedly involve the following responses:

- **The quality imperative**: investment in R & D and information systems; market research and quality design of goods and services; high-quality production of goods and delivery of services; an emphasis on sales and marketing
- **Information technology**: Investment in knowledge-based systems; development of all managers in the use of information to make decisions; decentralization of information and responsibility for executive decisions
- **Organizational upheavals**: The development of ways of managing the organizational changes resulting from acquisitions, mergers and diversification
- **Knowledge base**: The development of information systems easily available to employees; searching out and development of knowledge already existing within the organization; new relations with knowledge-based institutions; and an increase in the number of people operating at the boundary of the organization
- **Away from bureaucracy**: Giving power and responsibility back to the people who do the work; ensuring that the support systems meet their needs; reducing rules and formalization, and concentrating on acquiring, managing and delivering projects to the client's satisfaction.

These, then, are the likely strategic directions. What do they imply for the organization's management of its human resources? For it is only when human resource management is allied to the organization's business strategy − and is *seen* to be necessary to its success − that it becomes more than a minor administrative chore.

People

One message comes through loud and clear: all of the strategic thrusts of the 90s need quality people. What sort of quality people − can we buy them from Oxbridge or Harrods? If my analysis is correct, we are going to need:

- scientists, engineers and software people
- designers of goods and services
- marketers and salespersons who can operate in Europe
- managers who understand the uses of information technology and are willing and able to take decisions
- managers who understand how organizations work, and who can tolerate the ambiguity of differing and changing sub-cultures
- employees who can work at the boundaries of the organization and understand the environment they operate in
- employees who can work together in teams and give authority to whoever has the appropriate skills or knowledge
- employees who are willing and able to acquire new skills and knowledge
- employees who can reconcile their professional allegiance and their organizational membership, their commitment to their career, their job and their organization.

So human resource plans need to attract, retain and/or develop people like this. Where will they find them in the Britain of the 90s? Here are a few reasons why it will be hard to find them at all, in any of the traditional places:

- **Demography**: The number of school leavers in 1992 will be two thirds what it averaged in the 80s. This single fact makes a lot of present practices untenable. If we continue to expect nurses to start training at under 20 years of age, to be female, and to have the equivalent of 5 'O' Levels, the profession will need more than half the output of academically able female school leavers.
- **North and South**: Disraeli's one nation has gone for a burton long ago. The South-East is becoming part of Europe, with Londoners buying up property in Northern France in anticipation of the Channel Tunnel and 1992. It is also enlarging its boundaries, as East Anglia, the Midlands and Southern England as far as Bristol become commuter country. But the increasing concentration of

capital and business in the South-East has rendered half of the nation's human capital unavailable and impotent. The cost of housing in the South-East effectively prevents mobility of labour, even if Norman Tebbit's bike were as attractive a form of transport as he thinks it should be. Young people sometimes come to London desperate to find work, and finish up under the arches; families can't even contemplate a move.

- **Education**: Recent changes may well decrease the quality of education for the mass of the nation's children. They will certainly decimate the number of teachers — disillusioned London teachers are leaving in large numbers. In one regional survey of 30 schools, not a single teacher-trained physics graduate could be found. Physics, mathematics, foreign language, and design and technology teachers are the hardest of all to find.

  Lack of resources and lack of recognition have meant that even necessary changes — the introduction of the General Certificate of Secondary Education and the establishment of a National Core Curriculum — are having a rough ride. It is odd to try and create a system which educates all the nation's children to achieve something approaching their potential by cutting back on the resources it needs. It is also odd to prevent the broadening of the 'A' Level curriculum; compare a French Baccalauréat with the three 'A' levels of an English 18-year-old. At precisely the period in the nation's history, therefore, when it is *vital* that *all* the lower number of school leavers available are broadly educated and able to learn and develop, we have a disillusioned and despairing teaching profession and an unprecedented boom in private education.

- **Graduates**: Traditionally, organizations have used the social class and higher education systems to produce for them a set of intelligent employees destined to be scientists and engineers, other professionals (lawyers, accountants, etc) and general managers. This expectation is no longer justified. At the end of 1987, 9 per cent of jobs advertised for graduates were unfilled. Two organizations, GEC/

Marconi and Peat Marwick McLintock, look for more
than 1,000 graduates each per annum. The demand for
graduates is continually increasing, with retailing and
fast-food organizations joining in the hunt. Particular
shortfalls occur in information technology, mechanical
engineering, chemistry, accountancy, law and teaching.
From the trough of 1981, with the exception of a hiccup in
computing in 1986, demand has increased steadily, and
will continue to do so in the 90s. Projections of demand
indicate a requirement for 20 per cent more general
management trainees and scientists and engineers, and 17
per cent more professionals, by 1995.

What of graduate supply? Government projections are
for a general rise, flattening out in the mid 90s as the
demographic trough in school leavers makes itself felt,
but rising more steeply by the late 90s (see Appendix,
Table 1). The Government predicts that 20 per cent of the
relevant age group will participate in higher education by
then, as opposed to 14 per cent at present. Are these
predictions trustworthy? I don't think so, and what is
currently happening bears out my cynicism. Universities
have received almost static funding and student numbers
in recent years (see Appendix, Table 2). Specific and
highly selective increases in funding succeeded in increasing the output of graduates by 3 per cent in 1987 (well
below the increase in employer demand). But the indications are that the Government expects higher education
to get its support from other sources. Much effort is put
into acquiring short-term commercially oriented research
contracts from industry, running short courses or
promising to teach 'enterprise skills', whatever they may
be. The quality and number of graduates are bound to
suffer, as certain universities are designated 'teaching
only' in certain subjects and disillusioned academics take
the money and run, or go abroad to do their research.

Government expects increased numbers of women,
ethnic minorities and mature students to contribute to the
increased student participation rate. But why should

they? These groups are no more likely to participate in higher education as a consequence of present and intended policies. Within a year or two, students will probably be receiving loans rather than grants, a development likely to discourage working-class students even further (and ethnic minorities tend to be of lower socio-economic status). Part-time mature students aren't eligible for maintenance grants; they can't even claim tax relief for expenditure on their education. Government policy is to charge them cost fees and expect them to negotiate bank loans on the basis of the higher earnings they can expect after graduation! As for women, they now provide more than 40 per cent of the student body, and so a great increase in female applicants is unlikely.

But the decrease in applicants for specific subjects is most worrying of all. While employers say that they have no preferences as to degree subject for 40 per cent of their jobs, there are many jobs which do require specific training. Our embryo human resource requirements outlined on page 6 indicated the need for increased numbers of scientists, computer people, designers and linguists. Yet it is precisely these disciplines where applications have fallen. Between 1985 and 1987, university applications for physical sciences, languages, engineering and mathematical sciences all decreased by 9 per cent or more. Table 3 (see Appendix) is revealing of the recruitment problems for employers which inevitably result.

It is easy but mistaken to criticize foolish student choices. It may not be foolish at all to calculate that if you only managed to scrape through physics at 'O' Level because you were taught physics by the biology teacher, you don't stand much chance at 'A' Level. Indeed, you are probably being extremely hard-nosed, realizing that all graduates are in demand, so you might as well go for easier 'A' Level subjects which are taught by qualified people. Now physics and mathematics are required 'A' Level subjects for most engineering degrees and for all physics degrees. No wonder there are few science and engineering students – they have to sit the hardest subjects taught by the worst qualified staff. Ask any teacher, and they will say that the hardest 'A' Level subjects to pass are the long established ones: the natural sciences, mathematics, French, English and history. So what do most pupils want to study? Why, business and administration, which they often mistakenly believe will get them plum jobs in the City; in 1985–7 there was a 13 per cent increase in applications for this 'subject'.

Of course, we should not assume that because a student obtains a scientific or technological qualification, they will enter a related job. Far from it. The big accountancy firms, who employ more than 10 per cent of graduate output, positively welcome scientists and engineers. Some City firms are currently offering salaries of £16,000 to graduates, while retail and consultancy organizations give more than £12,000. Contrast the teacher of physics or the mechanical engineer, both of whom will be starting at well under £10,000. But then British culture has long undervalued the people who design and make things; it has also been fiercely anti-intellectual, and this has culminated in the current trivialization of education into the teaching of specific skills which will often be outmoded by the time pupils enter employment. What pupils and students need for themselves, and what their employers want of them, is the capacity and inclination to learn and keep on learning.

- **1992 Again**: We all know that the Single European Market in goods will come in the 90s. But what not so many are aware of is the open market in people. Government spokesmen have emphasized that the freedom to work throughout the European Community is an essential element of a genuine single market. Most professionally qualified people will be able to offer their services anywhere in the EC. Already, Dr Findlay can practise medicine in France, or James Herriot treat animals in Holland. Now, scientists and engineers, accountants and certain kinds of lawyers, systems analysts and programmers, will be occupationally mobile.

In no circumstances will they have to requalify — if there are marked national differences in qualifications, the worst that can happen is the requirement to serve a three-year 'apprenticeship' or take an aptitude test.

How will this new mobility affect us in Britain? Ask yourself a question that is rhetorical, so obvious is the answer. If you were a German or a Dutch engineer or teacher of physics at a school or university, would you come to Britain?

You are honoured and respected in your organization and your community. Frau Doktor Engineer has got a very good chance of getting on to the board. Herr Doktor of Physics has professional standing, a salary commensurate, and the physical and human resources to get his real job done properly. Is Britain likely to look very tempting?

Furthermore, with multi-nationals paving the way, many UK professionals will perceive advantages in living and working in the EC. There will not be an influx, but an exodus — designers to Dusseldorf, physicists to Freiburg, computer scientists to Cologne, engineers to Essen and mathematicians to Milan, all following crooks to the Costa Brava. Tax cuts in the top bracket won't retain them or attract the Europeans, since salaries aren't always competitive and quality-of-life issues are often as important as money.

To sum up: it is not merely that there is a mismatch between manpower demand and supply. Rather, demand and supply are careering in opposite directions at a very great rate of knots. In the 90s, organizations will need:

- more engineers, scientists and computer people
- more professionals
- more managers
- more technicians
- more designers, marketers and salespeople.

All of these people will need to be broadly educated, familiar with information technology, at home in Europe, equipped to understand organizational change, and capable of working together in teams. In other words, organizations will need more highly educated people.

Where will they get them from? Not from the schools: the demographic dip, and the lack of attraction of the teaching profession will see to that. Not from the universities: the number of graduates will stay constant, their quality will decrease, and there will be even fewer scientists and engineers. Not from the European Community: on the contrary, it will take away many of the people we've got now. Not from Scotland, Wales, the North, or Northern Ireland: they can't afford to move to the South. So what is there to do?

Chapter 2

Reactions to the Coming Crisis

Intimations of approaching doom and hints of worse to come have already prompted some rough and ready responses. These may be broadly summarized as:

- buy them
- make them
- recycle them
- select them
- contract with them.

Buying them

This tactic implies that you are in the market for a scarce commodity in competition with others. It also implies the belief that everyone has their price. If you buy something, you believe that you possess it. Often, you're not too sure what you wanted it *for*, but having spent that amount of money you have to convince yourself that it was worth it. One way of doing so is to show it off to make others envious; another is to use it as a symbol of status and success.

These assumptions and motivations seem to underlie the

frenzied attempts to persuade graduates or more senior
people to join one organization rather than another. Initial
graduate salaries are now 80 per cent of average male
earnings, a rise of 18 per cent since 1982. 'Golden hellos' of up
to £2000, together with extensive benefits packages, are being
offered by some City firms. One local authority even offered
to pay graduates a salary for the last three months of their
studies − if only they signed on the dotted line.

Organizations who court the gilded youth have to believe
that they are buying 'the best'. 'Golden hellos' can only cap
the cream; it's silver tops for the common or garden milk of
the graduate milk round. After all, it's not enough to have
more of something; you need to have more of the best. Only
then can you lay claim to excellence and exclusivity −
excellent organizations have to recruit excellent people.

The consequences of this strategy were recently made plain
in a television series about an Oxbridge college. Young people
with no idea of how organizations work or how most other
people live were supremely confident of their desirability and
worth in cash terms. It is not accidental that they were
Oxbridge students. For some organizations' definitions of
excellence are bound up with the pecking order of British
higher education. The pecking order concerned is that of
social desirability − to which universities do the rich and
famous prefer their children to go? Oxbridge − or, failing
that, Bristol, Exeter, Sussex or Durham. Certainly not to
those nasty big city universities, where they might meet just
about *anyone*.

Offering 'golden hellos' to the gilded youth from certain
universities points to the continued dominance of the class
structure in British society; any European, American or
Japanese can spot it a mile off. But the practice of 'buying the
cream' raises more important questions about purpose. We
need to ask such organizations what they want graduate
employees *for*. When they have stopped mouthing slogans
about 'excellence', 'cream' and 'commitment', the answer
might be something like this: we need Oxbridge people
because we need to maintain our image as a blue-chip
company which deals only with other blue-chip companies or

with those prepared to pay extra for the privilege.

This is part of the British disease which 1992 will cure painfully. While aristocratic accents still cut some ice in Boston or Hollywood, they cut no ice at all with the Germans, Dutch or Belgians, who merely find them harder to understand than BBC or American English.

Recent trends, however, soften this picture to some extent. Many large British firms have been broadening rather than narrowing their recruitment base in higher education. Many have recognized that, particularly in specific technical functions, polytechnic graduates are thoroughly good value. Much of the Oxbridge snobbery is now located in the merchant banks and in American and Japanese multinationals, who will soon learn better.

More generally, the strategy of 'golden hellos' and other inducements over and above the going rate is bound to fail in the longer run. As more and more organizations feel they have to buy a scarce commodity in competition with others, the stakes will be upped and upped. Before long, the bubble has to burst. Hard-nosed accountants will do their sums. They will discover that the gilded youth quite likes being bought; once corrupted, it will sell itself again without much thought. The costs of recruitment, inducements and salary may well start to exceed the benefits of the brief employment encounter. And we all know that it's the accountants who decide what happens.

Most of the research on turnover suggests that organizations usually over-emphasize the value of salary and perks in improving performance and retention. Instead of *assuming* that everyone is motivated primarily by financial rewards and perks, they should be spending more time finding out what employees *actually* expect from them. Different people at different life stages have different needs and wants, which implies that organizations will attract and retain people if they deal with them as individuals. It is the central argument of this book that it is only when organizations agree contracts with individuals which take account of their specific needs that they will be able to meet the human-resource challenge of the 90s.

Making them

This alternative strategy is particularly favoured where the aim is to produce more *managerial* talent. Indeed, the production of scientists, engineers and information technologists is hardly contemplated by organizations. They realize that the costs in equipment and staff are huge, and so they leave it to the polytechnics and the universities. Unfortunately, they contribute little to compensate the governmental underfunding and, understandably, don't see why they should. However, willingness to release employees for full-time (or even part-time) higher education as mature students is notably absent; organizations unfortunately seem to feel that this does nothing but make employees more attractive to competitors. Many of our students at Birkbeck College specifically request that they should not be contacted at their employment in case their organizations find out that they are studying!

As far as managerial training is concerned, we are currently witnessing a major initiative by the Charter Group of organizations. Spurred on by the Handy and the Constable and McCormick reports on management education, this aims to professionalize management. Employees will be encouraged to take diploma- and degree-level courses at specific early career stages, and will finish up as 'chartered managers'. Underlying this development is the belief that management is like any other profession: there are specific skills and knowledge on which it is based, and which can be assessed.

Unfortunately, there is no clear understanding of what these skills or competencies (to use the buzz word) really are. Nor is it evident that they can be assessed. The tasks that managers perform are many and varied. It depends on what level they are at in the organization, the function they are managing, and the sector they are in. It also depends on the identity of the organization itself; each organization has its own cultures within which managers operate, and the language, myths and manners of which they have to operate with. Henry Mintzberg agrees that the tasks may vary across levels and functions, but argues that they differ only in the proportion of the manager's time which is occupied by each sort of task. Hence the different competencies necessary to succeed in the tasks will differ in emphasis, argues Boyatzis (another management theorist), but will still be relatively few in number.

The real problem lies in the processes by which tasks are translated into the competencies supposed necessary for their completion. We have no clear theoretical understanding of higher-level skills and how they are organized. 'Strategic planning' or 'oral communication', for example, are so-called competencies which are in fact catch-all labels for a whole set of managerial tasks. They bear no particular relation to any theories about how people think. My daughter likes riding bicycles and horses, but it doesn't follow that there is a skill of riding which enables her to do so.

It is, therefore, hardly surprising that competencies have proved impossible to measure. The exercises used in managerial assessment centres are specifically designed to assess competencies. Based more or less closely on tasks from the job, each exercise is designed to assess several different competencies. For example, the well-known in-basket exercise (in which the assessee deals with a managerial in-tray) is designed to assess, among other competencies, those of prioritizing and delegating. Other exercises assess different competencies, but each competency is likely to be assessed by several different exercises. Now recent research in America and Britain has come up with a very awkward finding: assessments of different competencies within the same exercise are much more closely related than assessments of the same competency over different exercises! In other words, it is overall performance on the exercise which is being assessed, not the specific competencies. At the very least, this means that the competencies are not appropriately derived from the tasks.

Other recent British evidence casts doubt on the notion of a few key competencies common to all managerial work. The Institute of Manpower Studies carried out a survey of British companies which examined in detail their managerial assessment documentation: the forms they used for selection, appraisal, promotion and potential. They catalogued all the words denoting competencies, attributes, traits etc, and were amazed by the diversity of terms used (see Appendix, Table 4). Moreover, it became clear to them that the same term was used in very different ways by different organizations. It was as though there were organizationally defined competencies which varied according to sector and culture.

Isolating, defining and assessing underlying competencies, then, remains a daunting – and perhaps impossible – task. What we are left with is a huge variety of tasks that managers carry out in response to the expectations of others within and outside their organization. Their success in satisfying those expectations, in communicating their own and getting them met cannot be accounted for in terms of qualities or competencies within the manager. It has to be understood in terms of continuing relationships between the managers and those with whom they deal.

People's behaviour at work, in other words, is not only a result of the sort of people they are. It is part of a cyclical process, in which people act upon their own situation, for example, by putting forward a proposal for organizational change. Their superior may listen to and reject the proposal, which response will alter the manager him- or herself. As a consequence of this learning process, their next action for change may well take a different form. It follows that we cannot meaningfully assess managers in isolation from their organization.

More fundamental still, we may question whether there exists, except at very senior levels, a general managerial function. Many of our Continental competitors don't seem to think so. They employ all their highly educated employees in specific functional positions. The engineer who becomes production manager has had line experience and is then given training in production management.

The implication of all these doubts for the strategy of making managers is clear. Managers are made *throughout* their organizational careers, not at the beginning of them. Organizations still need to find high-quality staff to fill functional positions and to develop them later. The manufacture of managers in the absence of considerable functional and organizational experience is impossible. Attempts to teach management to school and university students appear faintly ridiculous.

So, making managers through general managerial training looks like being the wrong option, although that doesn't mean that the basic strategy of making people is mistaken. On the contrary, the shortage of graduates in the 90s suggests that organizations should be looking elsewhere. Since it is largely social class which predicts whether or not an adolescent goes to university, it follows that there is likely to be a great deal of talent available elsewhere. Agreed, 16- and 18-year-olds will be in very short supply too. But they are likely to be attracted to organizations which make it very clear that they are not second-class citizens, taking the slow track behind the graduate fast stream. Rather, their training and development should be carefully planned, in line with their own aptitudes and interests and with the organization's human-resource needs. Many more options are open to both parties than the technical specialization or general training scheme often followed by all graduates. Organizations must ask themselves *why* they are so hooked on graduates – is it simply that they are willing to let the education and class systems do their selecting for them?

Recycle them

Organizational careers are finishing earlier and earlier in the lifespan; golden hellos are matched by golden handshakes – often, these days, in a person's early or mid-fifties. The alternative is often demotion to a soft, welfare role like dealing with the charitable side or liaising with the universities.

Why should this be, when people of ability are in such short supply? The answer lies in the nature of organizational structures and careers. With the removal of tiers of middle management, and the slimming down of middle management generally, progress to senior management occurs earlier in life than it used to. If we suppose that 10 years is a reasonable period to occupy a senior management position, people aged 40 will continuously be knocking on the door of the 50-year-olds. In order to retain the 40-year-olds, into whose development a lot of effort has been put, senior management has to be moved out.

Of course, it is hierarchical organizations which suffer most from this syndrome. In such organizations the term 'career' is synonymous with promotion. Organizational worth and self-worth are defined in terms of level, and the power, status and perks that go with it. Career is construed as a ladder which you climb up rung by rung – and then fall off the top.

Another way of looking at careers is as a sequence of agreements between individual and organization. Instead of regarding its employees as human resources which it owns, the organization can come to view the employment relationship as a psychological contract which has to be periodically negotiated. By a psychological contract, we mean an agreement by organization and employee based on each party's expectations of the other at any particular point in time. Just as they assume that everyone has a price, some organizations seem to believe that everyone wants promotion. To discover otherwise involves lengthy and skilled consultation, in which the employees' expectations at each period of their personal lives are balanced with the organization's human resource plans in the light of its corporate strategy.

But organizational cultures don't change overnight. Many organizations with hierarchical structures and assumptions will be needing skilled people in the 90s. Why not bring back the 55-year-olds? Obviously there needs to be a period away from the organization, to indicate that they have indeed relinquished their senior position. Failure to ensure this gap is often the cause of trouble in the one case where people *are* kept on – as Chairman after being Chief Executive. How to use people who return in their own and the organization's best interests is a challenge to organizational bureaucracy. They certainly won't want to work the 60-hour week of their heyday. Many of them could be extremely helpful mentors to younger people, and avoid the dangerous confusion of mentoring with patronage. Since they would no longer be holding positions of power, they could concentrate on the other's and the organization's best interests and forget about empire building. But perhaps the most crucial potential role for the returner is as a boundary person, relating to other organizations.

When people return for second careers, organizations are gaining the benefits of a career's experience. But there is another group of employees upon whom organizations have spent resources for their recruitment, induction and training, and from whom they have yet to reap the benefits. They are parents. Many women, and a few men, leave their jobs in order to raise children. As a few far-sighted organizations have realized, parents aren't a lost cause. They can be assured of training and up-dating during long-term parenthood leave, and of re-introduction without their career progression suffering. Re-introduction may have to be gentle, and involve part-time rather than full-time work for a period. But if organizations cannot adapt to suit their employees' needs, they won't survive. They will retain administrative power in order to maintain a tidy male full-time bureaucracy; they will fail to see that market power has passed to their employees.

It's not as though organizations don't know what retired people and parents want. Retired people want to have their cake and eat it – and quite right too. They want the benefits of retirement and the stimulation of work. They want to do the things they've always wanted to do but never had the time for, while at the same time they want to continue to use their knowledge and skills, and retain the self-esteem that they get from being valued. So flexible part-time contracts are indispensable.

Parents need such facilities as nurseries *at work*. They need to be able to predict their hours of work, and they will find that some organizational practices are impracticable. They will not, for example, be willing to attend residential training courses; other modes of delivering training at work or at home will have to be devised. And they will have to be convinced that they stand just as good a chance of career development and promotion as the next person.

In general, organizations will have to be much more flexible in recruiting and retaining people from other potential recruitment souces. Handicapped people are often *better* at some work (rather than just not inferior) than those without handicaps. For example, there is some evidence to suggest that blind people are likely to make particularly good computer programmers.

Religious minorities will have to be catered for as well. A possibly apocryphal story recounts how a finance house lost the potential services of a brilliant Orthodox Jew because it could not agree to his returning home before nightfall on Fridays. More generally, are organizations prepared to make provision for dietary requirements and religious observance, or are devout people bound to work for their co-religionists? Indeed, are corporate cultures so resolutely male, Anglo-Saxon, anti-intellectual and secular that minority group members can't imagine themselves fitting in? How necessary are these cultural features to the organization's success? Are they not rather the historical products of our insularity, shortly to be rendered even more of a liability by the mobility of 1992 and the further growth of multinational organizations?

Select them

Rather than buying or making managers, many larger organizations are developing their selection procedures in a highly professional way, often using consultancy firms to help them do so. The rationale for this strategy is this: if organizations select people better suited to the job, then their push to improve quality will succeed, and employees are less likely to be dismissed or leave.

The selection strategy runs as follows:

• Attract as many applicants as you can, since the more you have to choose from, the better the choice
• Determine the most frequent, important and difficult tasks in the job by means of a job analysis

- Infer the skills and attributes necessary to complete these tasks satisfactorily
- Discover and apply methods of assessing these skills and attributes
- On the basis of these assessments, select those who are most likely to succeed at the job
- Evaluate the effectiveness of the selection procedure by seeing how well the assessments predict the actual performance of those selected; and by estimating the utility of the selection procedure in cash terms.

There is a considerable array of assessment methods available to organizations, and there is also a great deal of reliable research evidence about them. The matter about which there is most evidence is their criterion validity: that is, to what extent do each of them predict job performance? Recent research has cumulated large numbers of studies with different organizations (mostly in America) and have come up with a clear order of effectiveness in this respect. The best methods are assessment centres, tests of intellectual aptitude, job-sample tests and structured situational interviews. Assessment centres actually contain these other methods within them. Somewhat less effective is the use of scored biographical data, while tests of personality and the usual sort of interview are of relatively little use.

However, what must be noted is that none of these methods on their own predicts with a relationship of much more than .4 with performance (that is, they do not predict more than 16 per cent of the variability in performance). Therefore 84 per cent is not predicted. Even when complementary methods are used in combination, prediction is very seldom above .6 (36 per cent). These figures put a different complexion on claims to 'take the uncertainty out of selection' made by some unprofessional consultancy firms. What selection methods *can* do is increase the probability of selecting suitable people for the job. However, a small improvement in this probability can mean a very great improvement in productivity measured in cash terms. This is especially true where there is a large number of applicants, and a wide range of performance possible on the job.

Thus there are methods available which would, if used, result in a considerable improvement in job performance, and hence in quality of product or service. However, although some major organizations take the evidence seriously, most do not. A recent survey of the different methods used for managerial selection came up with the results in Table 5 (see Appendix).

It's clear that the most popular methods are certainly not the most effective, with the traditional interview retaining pride of place despite its poor validity. There may be good reasons for its survival as a favourite method, which I will discuss later. There is no good reason at all for the use of methods such as graphology and astrology, which have not been shown to predict job performance (although it is interesting that a large number of French organizations use graphology).

The overall picture of selection practice in the UK is certainly grossly at variance with professional practice, as the next chapter will argue. But it does not follow that the model selection procedure as advocated in the textbooks and described above is actually appropriate in the 90s. Indeed, the fifth strategy, that of *contracting*, is going to be preferable to selecting in the context of the sellers' market of the 90s.

Chapter 3
What Do Organizations Do Now?

Traditional pitfalls

At present, organizations often act as though they are in a
buyer's market, as indeed a few of them still are. They seem
to imagine that it is only they who have to make a decision —
whether or not to employ this applicant. If the applicant is
stupid enough to refuse their job offer, there are many others
equally well suited who will be more grateful.

This posture boosts organizations' morale enormously. It
enables them to maintain the belief that they are among the
blue-chip companies for which it is an honour to work. They
are misled by the huge volume of applications, which usually
just means that applicants are making multiple applications.
Many are attracted by glossy brochures which paint an
idealized picture of an organization caring but not paternal-
istic, offering responsibility with support, and providing
demanding but interesting and fulfilling work.

Having attracted a wide field, organizations then discard
the majority of applicants in a profligate and wasteful way.
For example, when recruiting graduates, they may discard at

least half on the basis of a rapid read of the application form and a subjective judgement. Then they discard half of those left on the basis of a half-hour 'milk-round' interview. Now both of these assessments are unreliable and invalid. They don't give the same results on two separate occasions, and they predict future job performance only slightly better than chance. So as many as 75 per cent of applicants have been discarded using assessment methods which are almost useless. Assume 4,000 applicants, of whom 1,500 receive a first interview and 600 go on to a second interview or an assessment centre. Thus 4,000 people have been reduced to 600 by an almost random method. Only if you believe you have an endless supply of eager applicants can you contemplate such waste. So the strategy can be seen as a selection strategy, but a highly inefficient one.

Organizations often forget that applicants have a decision to make as well. Despite the existence of long-term unemployment in certain occupations and among particular sections of the population, there are many applicants who can pick and choose even now, especially in London and the South-East. Technicians, engineers, programmers, analysts, secretaries, accountants, science and maths teachers, specialist nurses.... They are making decisions *throughout* the recruitment procedure – whether to apply, to accept an invitation to interview, to attend an assessment centre, to accept a job offer. On what are they to base their decisions? Many organizations *fail to provide the information* they need and see no reason to do so. In the 1990s this shortsighted negligence will prove fatal to any hope of attracting and retaining valuable human resources.

Typical personnel practice in the 1980s fails to inform. Brochures and advertisements are aimed at attracting applications, which is a very different matter. A common technique is to personalize the jobs so that potential applicants can identify with the characters presented. Youthful and attractive employees are pictured performing interesting technical or social tasks with mellow sunlight flickering on the office walls. Women engineers or black managers are pressed into public-relations service. There is likely to be little about supervision, career development or training. There will be nothing about the boring routine parts of the job, or the organizational culture and lifestyle. And problems will be avoided like the plague; the only exceptions are those organizations appealing specifically to the macho market – people who need to prove themselves really tough.

Interviews will follow if the applicant is pre-selected, although pre-selection itself is largely a lottery. If the applicants can't find out about the job or the organization, they don't know how to fill in the application form so as to succeed. The worst muddle of all is the open question: for example, why do you want to work for this organization? Knowing nothing about the organization whatsoever, applicants are apt to parrot back phrases from the brochure – 'because I want to work for the most advanced firm of Chartered Accountants in the UK'. The main thing to avoid is revealing ignorance about the job or the organization.

Having asked for a great deal of information, organizations don't know what to do with it. One of the reasons is that they don't know why it's asked for in the first place. Much of the material on an application form is really for subsequent administrative purposes, should the applicant be employed. Other questions cannot by any stretch of the imagination be related to the job. Why should young applicants be asked their parents' occupations? Why should a woman (or a man) be asked how many children they have? Qualifications and work experience act as proxy evidence for skills and aptitudes – the implication is that because you've been trained to do something (or have done it already), you must be good at it. All sorts of inferences are made, including inferences about motivation and personality. 'If they haven't bothered to find out about us, they can't be motivated to work for us.' 'If they can't produce a tidy application form, they are too disorganized to work here.' 'Trying to be funny, eh? – a bit cocky for us.' And so on.

Having passed the paper sift, our heroine makes it to the interview. Here at last is a chance to find out a bit more about what she is letting herself in for. How reassuring to be told that the purpose is 'for each of us to get to know the other better'. At least she can ask some questions from someone who appears to know. Not a bit of it. The unspoken rules of the game state clearly that the interviewer asks questions of the applicant, then invites her to ask questions about the job. Almost invariably these are crammed into the last five minutes. And they aren't real questions – they are the questions the applicant thinks she ought to ask in order to appear in a good light.

This happens because the purposes of the interview are hopelessly confounded. It cannot operate both as a selection device and as an information exchange. Both functions are fatally flawed. Selection is invalid because the interviewer picks people whom he likes. He likes people who are similar in some way to himself, and who appear to like him. Information exchange is curtailed into wild surmise – this interviewer is polite and friendly, so the organization will probably treat me well. Decisions get made on totally inadequate and often prejudiced information. The organization recruits in its own image – or, rather, in the image of its recruiters. And the applicant creates for herself a picture of the organization in the image of its recruiters too. No wonder many British organizations are conservative!

Trendy tools

What about the other methods of selection? Assessment centres and several kinds of psychological test are increasingly being used (in order of popularity): tests of personality; tests of aptitudes; assessment centres; and scored biographical data. Despite the potential value of most of these instruments, horror stories abound. Let's start with the ones about purchase. Probably the most frequent reason for buying a *psychological test* is because a competitor or a prestigious organization in another sector is using one. Coming up fast, though, is the oldest salesman's trick in the trade. Give a personality test which 'takes only five minutes and will solve all your human resource problems' to as senior a person as possible. Interpret his results to him so that he replies (as quite a few will), 'Why, that's amazing. That's me to a T.' He may even call in his secretary to confirm the accuracy of the 'reading'. When the director agrees to complete the questionnaire, the salesman licks his lips. When he calls in his secretary, he's already got the order form completed. And we sneer at astrologers.

But what about use? The most frequent strategy is to use psychological tests as screening-out devices. Psychologists are seen as those who deal with people who have something wrong with them. Tests, therefore, are devices which discover these problems. When test results are provided to selectors, a typical response is to say: 'Good, nothing unusual there, then.' Or, alternatively, 'Oh dear, she doesn't seem too bright. We'd better check that out in the interview.'

Assessment centres are the flavour of the month, or rather of the decade. They involve the assessment of applicants in groups, and the assessment is carried out by several assessors, usually of middle- or senior-management status. An essential component is exercises which are designed to assess the various attributes, qualities or skills which are considered necessary for the job. These exercises may bear a close resemblance to certain tasks in the job or they may be somewhat removed. The former ICT Assessment Centre for promotion to middle management was a job-sample. It contained an in-basket exercise which consisted of papers taken from actual in-baskets in the organization. The Royal Navy, on the other hand, has would-be officers leading groups across water-tanks using barrels, ropes, planks, poles etc, not a frequent task in today's Navy. While the exercises form a central part of the assessment-centre proceedings, tests of aptitude and personality, interviews and biographical data may also be used.

When all the information has been acquired, the assessors rate the applicants on the attributes. They then, usually after much discussion, arrive at a single overall assessment rating on which the selection or promotion decision is taken.

Now assessment centres are in principle very useful. The overall ratings are among the best predictors of subsequent performance on the job, along with job-sample exercises or tests of intellectual aptitude on their own. What's more, they have all sorts of additional spin-offs:

- They keep middle managers happy, because they feel they have control over who gets in and gets on, rather than leaving it to those woolly personnel people
- They give the said middle managers training and practice in assessing people
- They appear fair and above-board to applicants
- They can even help applicants to understand more about the job and self-select out if they wish.

This last benefit isn't too likely, though. If our heroine has survived paper sift and interview, she will have convinced herself that the job must be worthwhile. She can't have gone through all that hassle for nothing!

However, assessment centres don't always work out as well in practice as they ought:

- Consultants may set up exercises from 'off the shelf', rather than developing ones designed to assess the particular attributes needed for the job
- Assessors don't assess attributes anyway – they assess performance at the exercise as a whole (see page 17 above) and then subdivide it into attribute ratings because they're told to
- Up to 24 attributes are sometimes assessed, yet only 3 or 4 contribute to the overall rating. As a consequence, much information is lost
- The wrong information is often given the heaviest weight. Exercises and interviews are most influential in decisions, whereas psychological tests and biographical data may be as good or better predictors. Perhaps this is because assessors see and hear the applicants in the exercises and interview. They themselves make the ratings. Psychological tests are completed elsewhere, and marked by those trick cyclists
- Long group discussions about applicants have little impact on ratings, and are unlikely to result in better decisions

- Applicants may not have been told in advance what was going to happen at the assessment centre
- They may be given no feedback about their strengths and weaknesses, except what they overhear when the assessors talk about them 'quietly' among themselves
- Those successful at assessment centres may be marked out as high-fliers, thereby demotivating everyone else and producing self-fulfilling prophecies.

It's the old old story — potentially very helpful methods can be misused because their purpose isn't clear; because they are not part of an overall and well designed selection system; because the people who introduce them are incompetent; or because people who assess aren't properly trained.

Any worthwhile assessment method is unlikely to be cheap or quick to use. Yet these seem to be the main criteria for purchase. To be of any use, assessments have to be reliable and valid. Something which takes five minutes to administer is most unlikely to be either, since it samples such a tiny proportion of the applicant's behaviour. Yet how many managers know what reliability and validity are, let alone insist that they see the evidence for them before they purchase a test?

And now for the really way-out techniques. Some organizations admit to using graphology, one or two even astrology. The reason these methods are in use is because of the marketing skill of the practitioner and the gullibility of the organization. The practitioner's skills lie in discovering things about the person being assessed (often, in the first instance, the potential purchaser of the technique) apart from that 'gained' by the handwriting (or birthdate, or whatever). That is why the graphologist asks you to write down something composed by yourself, rather than merely copy a passage from a book.

Purposes and methods

Such crackpot techniques are relatively rare. Their use is of little significance in the context of the major problem with UK selection procedures: that they assume a buyer's market in the face of the overwhelming evidence that things are changing. Perhaps the continuous need to resort to the use of head-hunters who charge one-third of the annual salary of those they recruit will persuade companies to change. Perhaps the ultimate failure of their present systems to attract or retain suitable applicants may bring it home to them at last. But the facts are clear now: many of them treat their applicants with scant consideration. They continue to abuse the power that they derive from managing the selection procedure, in blissful ignorance that market power is slipping away from them fast.

We have looked at some of these abuses:

- Many organizations don't provide truthful information about the job or themselves
- They don't tell applicants what their assessment procedures are going to be like, or why they are appropriate and necessary
- They don't tell them what their assessments are, nor explain their decisions to accept or reject
- They use unreliable and invalid (and therefore unfair or random) methods in preference to better ones
- They keep applicants waiting before making a job offer, then expect a rapid response
- They ask intrusive or sexist questions which are none of their business
- Above all, in the interests of bureaucratic efficiency, they treat applicants *en masse* instead of individually.

When there are many more applicants than jobs, organizations can afford to treat selection as an obstacle course, a series of hurdles to be jumped before the applicant reaches the gates of Paradise and is admitted to the circle of the elect. When there are more jobs than qualified people to fill them, such an approach is useless.

Now all this may be a bit of caricature. Perhaps no single organization makes all the blunders I've listed. But underlying the somewhat lurid picture are some basic policy problems. Why do organizations pick up the latest assessment tool as the solution to their problems? Why do they ape the selection practices of bigger organizations? Why do they spend a lot of money attracting applications, then discard them randomly? We have already proposed one reason: they haven't yet fully realized that it's a seller's market; or if they have, they haven't yet *acted* accordingly. But there are other deep-seated reasons too.

Essentially, many organizations haven't integrated their human-resource policies and practices with their strategic plans. They haven't, for example, asked themselves what they want graduates *for*. The recommended professional practice in selection would urge a job analysis of the entry job and choose selection tools on that basis so as to predict immediate job performance. But performance at the entry-level job may not be what the organization is interested in.

For example, the accountancy firms use graduate entrants on fairly routine audit work, partly because the job has to be done, and partly because the professional accountancy institutions require it for qualification. But technicians can do the auditing, especially as it becomes computerized. What they *really* want graduates for is to resource the businesses of tax, insolvency, management consultancy and audit after they have qualified. And they also prefer home-grown partners who have come up through the ranks and absorbed the company culture.

However, in so many organizations, such insights and objectives fail to be translated into recruitment and selection procedures. Instead, they spend more and more time, effort and money on ineffective traditional procedures which bear little relation to their present, let along future, needs. Slogans and buzz words like quality and excellence are no substitute for the development of recruitment policies based on the recognition of a seller's market, the analysis of organizational careers, and predictions about how jobs are going to change.

To sum up:

● Organizations currently recruit and select as though they were in a buyer's market
● Currently prevalent pre-selection and interview techniques are unreliable, invalid and wasteful

- Sounder methods, when used, are not always employed to the best advantage
- Little information or consideration is given to applicants
- These errors are due to a failure to integrate recruitment into a human resource strategy in a seller's market.

Chapter 4
A Radical Response

Better selection is still inadequate

The previous chapter presented an alarming and doubtless somewhat exaggerated picture of the awfulness of current recruitment and selection procedures. It's just possible, though, that you may have recognized a few shortcomings in your own organization from among the long list of sins of omission and commission. How can they be remedied?

One response is to maintain that these shortcomings are basically technical ones. The procedure described in Chapter 3 is a very poor selection procedure which needs to be improved. All the tools are available, and what is required is a thorough professionalization of the whole process:

- Instead of vague slogans of excellence, or the ideal managerial candidate, we need careful job analysis
- Instead of the random reduction of application forms by guesswork and interview, we need to develop biodata scoring schemes and structured interviews based on the job analysis
- Instead of second interviews with more senior people, which are likely to be yet more idiosyncratic in content and style, we need assessment centres designed on the basis of the job analysis

- All these methods will require the assessment of competencies or skills, which will have been inferred as necessary on the basis of the job analysis.

Now these would be the recommendations of most soundly based management consultants and occupational psychologists. They will very probably result in improvements in job performance, especially for jobs which have changed little. They will prove to be highly cost-effective if evaluated properly; in the short term, they are just what many organizations appear to need.

However, they are inadequate to the challenge of the 90s. We do not need to become more technically competent; we need to redesign our systems from top to bottom. We should not be trying to select more effectively, but to change the mode from *selecting* to *contracting*.

There are two reasons why such a radical change is necessary. The first is the changing nature of jobs and organizations; and the second is the labour market's change from a buyer's to a seller's market.

Outdated views of work and organization

We've already mentioned one or two shortcomings of the assessment of competencies in Chapter 2. Let's recapitulate them now, since they give us a lead into the nature of job and organizational change in the 90s. We noted that it has proved very difficult to identify key managerial competencies, and almost impossible to assess them properly. We need to ask why such an apparently straightforward task has proved so difficult. I will argue that it is because the task attempted is the wrong one. It is a task based upon outdated assumptions about the nature of jobs and organizations.

What are these false assumptions?

- That jobs are relatively static; therefore an analysis of the job as it is can be the basis for selecting and training people for the 'same' job in the future
- That jobs consist of a set of tasks which can be dis-

tinguished from each other and characterized by such features as their difficulty, important and frequency
- That jobs can be objectively analysed into their tasks
- That the tasks require personal competencies alone for their successful completion
- That organizations consist of individuals occupying a clear set of jobs, each of which is described by the tasks it involves
- That performance can and should be measured objectively, and at the level of the individual job-holder.

All of these assumptions are derived from a historic view of organizations and how they work. Essentially, they are based on manufacturing or business organizations in which the product or service provided did not change very much over time. To use Herb Simon's distinction, most of the work and decisions involved were programmable rather than non-programmable. You could in principle write programs which specified the alternative causes of action appropriate to achieve desired outcomes in particular situations. Indeed, principle has been transformed into practice with the auto-mation of many manufacturing and office procedures.

Now there are still organizations or parts of organizations where these conditions apply. But they are becoming less and less frequent, at all levels in the organization. Even if there are appropriate strategies or rules that can be followed, these can seldom be boiled down to specific actions. Some of the attempts to do so strike us as quite ridiculous, the 'Have a nice day' syndrome in the service industries being a good example. Instead of training staff to discover the customer's needs and try to meet them, some service-sector companies train them in specific parrot-like behaviour: 'When you greet people, say, "Hi there, welcome to Junk Food, Sir or Madam." ' Only when customers start objecting to being treated as sexually indeterminate does the stupidity of this approach strike Junk Food's management.

The point, though, is that the job of the Junk Food employee consists more in relating to people than in per-forming manual actions upon materials. As the service sector increases in size and staff relative to manufacturing, so more and more jobs require employees to relate to customers or clients and try to understand and solve their problems. To take another example, the technical competence of systems designers who produce elegant solutions is in less demand than the relational skills of understanding what clients want, helping them to appreciate how to use the system, and then adapting it more closely to their needs. This job of systems trouble-shooter is non-programmable. If it were programmable, it would certainly have been programmed into the system as designed!

Thus, more and more work involves understanding individual clients' problems and helping them solve them. In this sense, everyone's work is becoming more 'professional', since one of the characteristics of professional work is the unique relationship between professionals and their individual clients. More generally, we can conclude that work on behalf of one's organization is going to require the establishment and maintenance of relationships based upon the external client's needs and problems. It will consist of a continuous and changing *process* rather than a set of repeated tasks.

The same is true of work within the organization. Bureaucracy is slowly giving way to adhocracy as a preferred structure for organizations. As a consequence, employees perform a series or different roles as they are members of different project teams (either simultaneously or successively). Instead, therefore, of formally reporting and being reported to in accordance with line responsibilities, employees are required to nurture and sustain a wide variety of relationships. A manager may be a creative catalyst in one project team, monitor of progress in another, and responsible for implementation and resource-gaining in yet another.

Instead of conceptualizing a job as a set of tasks, we are having to construe it more and more as a set of relationships: relationships with clients and relationships with colleagues. Consequently, the idea of objectively quantifying and assessing performance is a mistaken one. At any point in time, our manager's performance will be assessed by different people in different ways, because they will each have their own point of view. Colleagues in project team A will appreciate his or her creative contribution to problem-solving, while the client tries unsuccessfully to persuade our manager to explain clearly what lines team A is working on. Moreover, as relationships within and, indeed, membership of teams change, evaluation of our manager changes too, since he or she is now in a different set of relationships.

Organizations have a great readiness for placing responsibility for outcomes upon individual employees. This is why they try to claim that results depend on the extent to which employees possess certain key competencies. At the same time, they realize that the nature of work is changing. They appreciate its wide variety and the continuous development that managers require. The consequence is a list of required competencies in managers which positively bursts at the seams. They expect initiative, creativity, commitment, independence, flexibility, strategic vision...

What they are doing, in fact, is putting their organizational-development needs on to individuals. Flexibility and initiative are not qualities located within individuals. Rather, they are statements about how the organization intends to survive and flourish in its environment. They imply that the organization needs to develop new products or services, cultivate new customers or clients, and achieve these ends largely by the use of its present members. The implication of the use of the words 'flexibility' and 'initiative' as personal attributes is that it is the individuals' own responsibility to achieve these outcomes: 'If only we recruit and select people with these qualities, we can leave it to them.'

But organizations, if they are anything at all, are ways of coordinating the activities of individuals to achieve objectives. It is not individuals but groups of people in relationship with one another who achieve organizational ends. It is therefore the quality of these relationships between people, the process of mutual giving and taking, the variety of contributions from each to all, that are crucial. The implication of all this is the need for a wide variety of people in the organization, not for organizational cloning. Organizations need people of different interests, styles and aptitudes if they are going to have effective work groups.

If what I have just said represents the way work and organizations are changing, then all the assumptions under-lying professional selection procedures are mistaken. In summary:

- Jobs involve continuously changing relationships rather than static tasks
- Performance is subjectively evaluated by those to whom one relates, both internally and externally
- Competencies are not attributes of individuals but statements of organizational policy
- Organizations do not consist of aggregates of individuals, but of developing relationships.

Improved and more professional selection as presently understood doesn't seem to be the whole answer. If you can't analyse the job into tasks, then you can't infer the attributes required. If organizational performance depends upon re-lationships, then individual assessment isn't the answer. It looks as though we need a more radical approach.

The seller's market and the psychological contract

The other reason for proposing change is the labour-market trend of the 90s. From the trough of demand for graduates and skilled staff in 1981, the pendulum has swung, and it is now a seller's market. The market power is with the applicant, not with the organization. The applicants have the decisions to make as organizations compete for their services. This swing of the pendulum has profound implications for recruitment and selection, but organizations don't appear to have thought these through yet.

Essentially, if applicants more than organizations are the decision-makers, they will have to have good grounds for taking their decisions. Just as organizations in their selection mode feel the need for information upon which to base decisions of acceptance or rejection, so too do applicants. Given this *mutual* need for information and its exchange, the balance of power in the relationship has to shift. At present, the organization retains and uses its administrative power over the applicants. It often leaves them in ignorance about the job, the organization and the selection procedure itself. Such withholding of information is an abuse of administrative power. But the ultimate power is the market power of the applicants. So the degree of abuse of administrative power by organizations is likely to be reflected in the market decisions of applicants − they will simply opt out if they are treated badly.

How then are we to characterize the recruitment and selection systems of the 90s?

- There must be a surrender of administrative power by the organization so that the power relations in the procedure reflect the balance of market power
- The procedure itself should be considered as a developing relationship between the parties which *either* may break off
- This relationship is not divorced from the subsequent relationship after the employment contract; rather, the latter is a development of the former.

Chris Argyris, the famous American organizational psychologist, came up with a highly relevant concept in the early 1950s which has received little attention since. It is the idea of the *psychological contract* between organization and employee. As distinct from the employment contract, the psychological contract is not always explicit, and it certainly doesn't possess any status in law. The psychological contract isn't static and once-for-all. At any given point in time, it represents the understanding between the two parties in terms of what they expect of each other. Employees will have certain expectations about how the organization should treat them; the organization in turn expects various things of the employee. Each has to decide the extent to which they will fulfil the other's expectations, and the other needs to be satisfied with this degree of fulfilment. Otherwise, if the gap is too large, the other will exit. Employees will quit if the organization expects more than they are prepared to give, or if it fails to meet their expectations by a long way. The organization will seek to rid itself of employees who fail to meet its expectations, or ones who expect too much of it. (Of course, other factors will also be involved in quitting or dismissal − the labour market, for example.)

Thus, the psychological contract at any given time is a snapshot of a continuing process. That process is essentially one of communication and negotiation. The parties have to indicate to each other what their respective expectations really are. They also have to reveal the extent to which each is prepared to meet the other's expectations, so they can negotiate accordingly.

This is essentially the nature of career development. Career development seeks to reconcile the expectations and interests of the individual with those of the organization. A woman might seek to undertake the rapid sequence of jobs considered necessary for a management trainee somewhat earlier in her organizational career than usual. This would permit her to occupy a single position for a longer period in her late 20s as she rears a young family. The organization might agree, on condition that it could place her in a multi-faceted position for that period so that she continues to develop her skills and experience. Such a position could become vacant anywhere in the UK, so she must be prepared to move home to accommodate the organization's expectations.

Now that example was taken from an employment situation. What I am suggesting is that this idea of the psychological contract is actually applicable from the very start of the relationship between organization and employee. Applicants have expectations about how the organization will treat them before and after the employment contract is signed. Organizations have expectations of the applicants' behaviour, both as applicants and subsequently as employees. It follows that the recruitment and selection procedure may be seen as a process of psychological contracting. The organization tells the applicants what it expects them to do and how it wants them to act, both as employees and during the selection procedure itself. Likewise, the applicants can let the organization know what their expectations are about the treatment they will receive at its hands, as applicants and employees.

There may be mismatches:

- between the organization's expectations of how applicants should behave and applicants' expectations of how they themselves should behave
- between applicants' expectations of how the organization should treat them, and the organization's expectations about how it should treat them.

Now the psychological contract consists of the condition of the relationship at any one point. There may be a mismatch of the first type above. The organization might expect the applicant to undergo a psychological test of personality without being told why or receiving the results; or it might indicate that it wanted the applicant to undergo a fairly lengthy training course in information technology within the first 9 months of employment. In neither case did the applicant expect to have to undertake these tasks. What is he or she to do? There are three basic alternatives. The applicant can:

- change her behaviour to accede to the organization's expectations: take the test, or agree to undertake the training
- seek to change the organization's expectations: give them the results of an interest inventory already completed and understood, or suggest putting off the training for a year or two and letting a brief IT familiarization course suffice.
- quit the selection process with this organization and apply elsewhere.

There can also be mismatches of the second type, between the applicants' expectations of how the organization should treat them and the organization's expectations of the same. The applicants might expect an informative description of the job they have applied for, or a mixture of sound supervision with some autonomy in their work. The same three alternatives then face the organization. It can decide to give them what they want, it can try to persuade them that they don't really want it, or it can terminate the relationship by rejecting them. It can, of course, also reject them because it believes that it can't – rather than won't – meet their expectations.

So the selection process can be seen as part and parcel of the psychological contracting which goes on throughout an individual's career. Even before an employment contract is offered or signed, the parties are establishing a relationship. They are telling each other about themselves, and what they expect of each other. They are bargaining and contracting about the future. Putting it another way, the career development process begins as soon as the organization advertises the job. It's merely that at the selection stage both parties are more likely to quit the relationship than they are later.

This conceptualization of the selection process fulfils the requirements of the 90s. It recognizes the changed nature of work and organizations by concentrating on the relationship between organization and individual. It is only when this relationship is soundly established that organizations can hope to use their employees as flexibly as they would like. It also recognizes the market power of the applicants – they want a contract by negotiation, not a key to the Pearly Gates. The idea of the psychological contract is in marked contrast to the strategy of better selection, which implies the jumping of a sequence of hurdles, at each of which the applicant runs the risk of being rejected by the organization. It fails to recognize that the applicant can similarly reject the organization. It also fails to allow for the modification of expectations which is part of negotiation, and which precedes agreement and commitment.

Most important of all, perhaps, the traditional selection approach ignores the question of the *communication* of expectations. It certainly requires the applicants to give a great deal of information about themselves. But it gives them little chance to learn about the organization's expectations of them or to reveal their own expectations regarding working life. What, then, must each communicate to the other in order for a worthwhile psychological contract to be established? We need to split this into two separate questions. What do the applicants need to know? And what do organizations need to know? These are the subjects of the next two chapters.

Chapter 5

What Do Applicants Need To Know?

If psychological contracting is to work, both parties have to tell each other what it is they expect. Only then can they negotiate meaningfully about any differences between them. But, first, each has to understand what it is that the other needs to know. What do applicants need to know?

What is the job like?

Recently, many local-authority employers have started sending detailed job descriptions together with the application form. In so doing, they are telling applicants a lot more than many organizations. But such lists of tasks and objectives are noteworthy for what they leave out. They say nothing about how the job is typically carried out, or how objectives are normally attained. They don't specify the skills or knowledge required. They don't mention the different taskmasters who will be expecting different things of the applicant. They state to whom the applicant will report, but they don't say what supervision or support they will receive.

So what else might an applicant want to know? There is so much more to organizational life than the current tasks of the job:

- What are the unspoken expectations? Unswerving commitment, to use the current favourite word (often a euphemism for subordinating all other interests and values to those of the organization)? Working till nine at nights, and being prepared to move home at a moment's notice?
- How will their performance be evaluated, and what will be the outcome of such evaluations?
- What are the possible directions for career development, and how are such movements up or across managed?
- How much discretion will they have, and how far are decisions decentralized?
- Who really holds the power and what are the key power groupings?
- What does the organization believe to be its basic mission, or isn't the culture a missionary one?
- If not, what are the key values of the culture, and how are they expressed? Is it a very masculine culture, with stereotyped masculine 'virtues' such as decisiveness or ambition considered as desirable managerial characteristics?
- How does the organization deal with conflict, and what are the means of defending employees' rights?
- What are the organization's strategic plans and likely directions? How are the key factors in its environment likely to change?

Much of all this the organization itself may not know. Nevertheless, its overriding task is to help the applicants decide whether the organization's expectations and their own are reasonably compatible; and whether they think they are capable of doing what's expected of them. Here are some methods for doing so.

The first is some sort of *realistic job preview*. This can take various forms: a few written case studies of recently joined employees and their work; a video or film using cinema verité

Publications Department
Institute of Personnel Management
IPM House
Camp Road
Wimbledon
London SW19 4BR

IPM INSTITUTE OF PERSONNEL MANAGEMENT

Thank you for buying this book. We hope you will find it both useful and interesting. We would be grateful if you could return this postcard (post-free) and answer the following questions:

1. How did you find out about this book?

a) Found it in a bookshop ☐ if so which shop?_____

b) Read a review ☐ if so, which paper or magazine_____

c) Saw an advertisement ☐ if so which paper, journal or magazine?

_____

d) IPM Digest ☐
e) Personnel Management ☐
f) Harrogate Conference ☐
g) Required reading list, if so for which exam?

h) Other_____

2. Are you a member of the Institute of Personnel Management? ☐ Yes ☐ No

3. If you would like to receive a copy of our catalogue of publications, please write your name and address below

Name: _____

Address: _____

_____

_____

techniques; the 'shadowing' of a present job incumbent for part of their working day; a visit to observe or actually participate in the organization's work; some job-sample or training sample exercises; and the opportunity to talk to present job incumbents without being assessed while you are doing so. All these techniques result in applicants' expectations of the job becoming more realistic (which usually means less glowing). The consequence is that many self-select out, realizing that the organization's expectations and their own are incompatible. Consequently, there is lower turnover among those who are selected, and employees are much more committed to the organization.

Some of the methods mentioned above involve applicants actually attempting some of the tasks of the job. As a result, they can discover not only what it involves, but also how good they are at it. Among the UK organizations using some form of realistic job preview are J. Sainsbury's, who offer graduates the opportunity to try out job-sample exercises to discover what being a retail manager involves.

Another recently developed tool is the *job-knowledge inventory*. This is essentially a series of questions about the job to which applicants respond in questionnaire format. They are then immediately given the answers to the questions, and so can observe the extent to which they were mistaken. A questionnaire item might be as follows: 'A navy pilot has little routine report writing to do: true or false?' The fact that it is false is immediately brought to the applicants' attention. As this example suggests, the Royal Navy is one of the UK users of job-knowledge inventories. This technique is in marked contrast to a typical interviewer's ploy — to ask the applicants job-knowledge questions to see if they have done their homework. This is taken to indicate motivation to work in the occupation or organization. It results in the ludicrous situation of both parties at the interview trying to ask questions of each other about the job.

These explicit and conscious attempts to inform applicants are in marked contrast to many brochures, which are designed to attract them. They are a great improvement on desperate guessing based on what questions the application form asked,

how likeable the interviewer was, or how long the organization kept them waiting before making a job offer.
Unfortunately for the organization, applicants may not trust
them as sources of information. They are far more likely to
believe reports from friends or family, or from other sources
perceived to be more disinterested. *The only way to bridge
this credibility gap is to establish a relationship of trust.* Such
a relationship will depend on the organization's existing
reputation, and on the applicant's conducting the whole
employment negotiation with an individual recruiter. An
alternative source of trustworthy information is a union or
staff-association representative, or a young employee instruc-
ted to answer all the applicant's questions honestly.

If applicants need to know how capable they are of doing
the job as well as what it's like, then a major source of
information is the organization's own estimate of their
capability. If organizations are professional about their
assessments, they will base them on a job analysis. They will
assess the attributes, skills and knowledge necessary to
perform the job as presently defined satisfactorily. Indeed, if
they have taken on board the points I made in Chapter 4, they
will assess for the job of the future rather than the job of the
present. Either way, if some assessments occur early in the
selection procedure, knowledge of their own performance in
relation to the performance level required can enable
applicants to self-select out at this point. This saves their own
self-esteem and the organization expense.

Computerized assessment systems can take this process
even further. Suppose applicants have undertaken various
assessments typically used by organizations (for example, a
test of intellectual aptitudes) and have stored this information
in their own file under their own control. Then they can decide
whether or not to apply in the first place to a particular
organization on the basis of the level of aptitudes the
organization says it requires for a particular job; only if they
apply do they need to release the assessment data.

At present, many organizations fail to inform applicants
what they are assessing, let alone what the assessments are.
This is often because they have no good reason for making

these assessments, or because they are aware they are un-reliable and biased. The consequence is not only that applicants miss out on potentially useful information; they are also more likely to reject an organization which is unwilling to explain what it is doing and why.

What is the selection procedure like?

This brings us to the second area where applicants need information from the organization: the nature of the selection process itself. If the relationship with the organization is to develop from the very beginning, applicants need to know what to expect. Then they too, as well as the organization, can opt out if they find the relationship untenable. They may be unwilling to answer intrusive questions on an application form which takes two hours to complete or in a personality test when their relationship to the job is (to put it mildly) unclear: 'Do I like gay parties? What sort of a question is that?'

They will particularly want to know what to expect if they are to submit themselves to a lengthy procedure at an assessment centre. What will I be asked to do, and why? What is the organization looking for, and how does it assess it? Which parts of the assessment centre involve assessment, or am I under scrutiny when I'm eating my breakfast? Among UK organizations which take care to familiarize applicants in advance is the Civil Service Selection Board's assessment centre for administrative-grade officers.

Many organizations appear to believe that if they tell applicants what they are looking for and how they intend to assess it, applicants will somehow deceive them by presenting themselves in a false light. The reverse is in fact the case: when applicants *don't* know how they are expected to behave, the organization's selection decisions may be made on the basis of the applicants' ignorance of the rules of the game rather than their suitability for the job. The application form and the interview are prime examples. Applicants should know that it is important to fill up the sections where open-ended questions are asked on the form. They should be aware that interviewers like to be in charge of interviews and will expect applicants to wait until they are invited to ask questions. If they break these rules, inferences will be drawn about the sort of person they are, since rule-breaking behaviour always makes us wonder. (What do we think when the shop assistant asks us if we're happily married or whether our souls are saved?)

Another important piece of information applicants want is why they have been rejected. This information will be of great help to them in their search for other employment. Possibly through fear of being sued, most organizations send a brief letter of rejection. Many fail even this elementary test of courtesy.

Rejection can be very useful to applicants. It can given them feedback regarding their strengths and weaknesses as far as the job in question is concerned. They can then adapt their job-searching strategy accordingly. However, all too often rejection results in a loss of self-esteem. While one or two rejections can be attributed to the stupidity or poor selection procedures of organizations, more result in self-attribution for failure: I must be useless if everyone thinks so. Yet organizations spend their time and money attracting as many applicants as they can, so many of them will obviously be unsuitable and doomed to rejection. Self-selection out before application or at an early stage in the procedure helps people retain their self-esteem.

This brings us on to a third area of knowledge which applicants need to possess. One part of the equation is what the organization will expect of them in the job; a second is what it will expect of them in the selection process itself. But a third is required before applicants can take worthwhile decisions: knowledge about themselves.

What sort of a person am I?

Some knowledge about the self has already been referred to in this chapter. It is the knowledge about one's own capacity to do the job, which can be obtained from some of the tools of selection like tests of aptitude and job-sample tests and exercises. But there is a great deal more which applicants need to know about themselves if they are to match themselves appropriately with an organization.

One important concern is the relationship of their assessed capacities to their sense of their own ability to do the job. Putting it another way, how do their own views of whether they can do it fit in with the assessments of others? Since our belief in ourselves has a strong potential to motivate us, applicants and organizations are likely to benefit if applicants are a little more confident than others believe they have reason to be. On the other hand, there is a related feeling about the self which may not be so beneficial. We differ in the extent to which we think what happens to us is our own responsibility or is determined by something or someone outside our own control. Many organizations are happy to employ those with a highly developed sense of responsibility, although such people can be crippled by self-criticism when things go wrong.

There are other aspects of the applicants' views of themselves which are of equal importance when it comes to deciding whether or not to join an organization. One is our future selves:

- How do we see ourselves in five or ten years' time?
- What do we expect to become?
- What would we like to become?
- What is it possible that we might become?

All these constructions of their futures are of profound importance for applicants. They will be matching against them what the organization has told them about three things:

- its plans for its own future
- its plans for their careers and
- its culture and values.

A major accountancy practice may be expanding and diversifying rapidly. Instead of producing accountants who are involved in audit and tax services to clients, its greatest increase per annum in its employees is among management consultants, most of whom are not accountants. It is changing from being a professional bureaucracy to a multifaceted commercial business. It plans to offer more varied opportunities to its employees, but with much greater risk than in a safe professional niche. The acquisition of totally new skills rather than the periodic brushing up of professional knowledge will be required. More responsibility for attracting and managing business projects will be laid on individuals, and they will get on or get out. Instead of a steady professional progression to a partnership, starting on a pittance and finishing up with partnership and profits, there is jam today, but you have to dig deep and fast to get it and it can slip off your plate very easily. As a consequence, people are starting to work twelve-hour days as a matter of course.

Applicants to such an organization have to match this organizational future with their conception of their own future.

- If they expect to have a family and be involved with it
- If they want to become highly technically competent professionals
- If they dread the possibility of having no time or energy left for anything other than work,

then their future selves and the organization's likely expectations of them are mismatched.

There are more immediate concerns too. Applicants need to know what their own value priorities are. Pacifist engineering students have been known to apply to organizations manufacturing armaments! This is just as likely to be due to lack of awareness of their own feelings about producing weapon systems of immense destructive capability as to ignorance of the organization's products. Such obvious contradictions are perhaps infrequent. However, applicants should know whether they are prepared to design, make, market or sell goods or services which people don't need or which may even do them harm. They will have to decide whether their need for personal achievement is so much higher than their need to form relationships with others that they are prepared to work for an organization where dog eats dog and the Devil takes the hindmost.

Perhaps most basic of all, applicants need to know how flexible their view of themselves is. Are they likely to become more self-confident? Are they going to be willing to change their value priorities? Are they absolutely insistent on starting a family in their twenties? Can they see themselves as power brokers rather than professionals?

If they see themselves as willing and able to change in these profound and basic ways, then they may tolerate a considerable mismatch between themselves and the organization. Similarly, if they believe themselves capable of adapting the organization to themselves, as many senior executives do, then good luck to them. But, in general, self and organization should not be too incongruent; research shows that people describe themselves and the organizations they would like to work for by using the same adjectives!

The implications of self-knowledge are considerable. From such immediate concerns as 'Am I prepared to travel widely?' and 'How much close supervision do I want or need?' through to visions of oneself in ten years' time, a developed self-awareness is required. Many methods and tools are available to help people develop such knowledge:

- self-administered questionnaires about interests and values
- life-line exercises projecting ourselves into the future
- group discussion and individual counselling with careers advisers, particularly for young people.

For the more mature, the opportunity to step back, reflect and see oneself in the context of society, one's occupation, organization and personal relationships is beneficial and illuminating. Yet such opportunities are consistently being denied to people. Career services to schools, colleges, and higher education have been cut back. Organizations often fail to see the benefit in self-development for their employees. In an era of continuous organizational change, the need for parallel self-development has barely impinged on the collective consciousness. And then we are surprised that people suffer stress!

To sum up, applicants need to know:

- what the job is going to be like
- what the organization is going to be like
- the nature and purpose of the selection procedure
- their own abilities, values, intentions, aspirations and adaptability.

Chapter 6

What Do Organizations Need To Know?

We may start with one or two things they *don't* need to know. According to an interviewee in a recent investigation of young women's experiences in their first job, 'Every single interview I was asked if I had a steady boyfriend.' Another remarked: 'I'm not engaged but I wear a ring on my engagement finger. The ring was commented on one way or another in every interview I attended.'

About themselves

What they *do* need to know is considerably less trivial. To state the obvious: they need to know all the things that the applicants need to know, so that they can tell them what the job and the organization are like and are likely to become; the purposes and procedures of the selection process; and the expectations of applicants. They need to know these things because they need to tell the applicant about them (or at least about the first two).

But there is a more basic reason. Both parties need to know the same things in order to be able to take mutually acceptable decisions. The selection process of the 90s can't be construed as the organization acquiring information about the applicant and taking a decision on that basis. It will rather be a relationship in which all information is exchanged, negotiations are engaged in, and commitments may be made. Alternatively, the relationship will be broken off at some point, preferably by both parties and by mutual consent.

What do organizations need to know about themselves, and the jobs they are offering? They have to have a clear idea of where they would like to go, and how they might get there. Such strategic plans will have as a major component a human-resource plan. This will not merely be concerned with estimating the number of employees required in existing jobs. It will concentrate on what jobs will have to be like in five or ten years' time in order to cope with organizational and environmental change.

Some of the major clearing banks did such an exercise before the introduction of information technology, and realized the radical changes in jobs at all levels which were implied. Given the additional need to sell financial services in competition with other business organizations, banks have been forced to formulate career-development plans for staff which recognize that jobs will be quite different in the future.

It follows that the traditionally recommended good practice of conducting a job analysis on present incumbents will not be sufficient. Analysis has also to be made of the jobs of the future, in so far as this is possible. It will certainly be completely impossible if the organization has no corporate stategic plan or human-resource plan which follows from it. In the absence of such plans, all that organizations can say about the personal attributes required for the jobs of the future is that they involve 'flexibility' or 'adaptability', implying the willingness and capacity to acquire new skills and knowledge and play new roles. But, as I argued in Chapter 4, they are thereby putting onto employees all the responsibility for what they themselves should be doing. They are translating the responsibility for planning organizational change, which is primarily that of senior management, into a set of personal qualities. They are individualizing what is essentially corporate.

It is hard enough to derive the required attributes from analyses of existing jobs, and to assess them. How much more difficult to do so for the jobs and careers of the future! Yet perhaps these attempts to specify particular attributes can be dispensed with. What organizations need to concentrate on is what jobs will be like, what the organization will be like and, consequently, what the likely career pattern within the organization will be. Career development in the 90s will become a process of reconciliation, between the anticipated needs of the organization and those of the individual, achieved through negotiation.

The implications of all this for the selection process will be explored in the next chapter. The organization will have to be aware of the connection between its future plans and its selection process, because it will need to communicate them to applicants. It is because the organization wishes to develop in a particular direction that it intends to run its selection process in the way it does. Applicants can only understand the need for particular procedures if they are aware of what they are *for*.

About applicants

What, then, does the organization need to know about applicants? At present, they often require a very great deal of information.

- Is it all necessary?
- How is it used?
- On what basis is it gathered?
- Who owns it?

The selection process of the 90s implies that both parties share the same information in order to match their expectations. This means that organizations have to discover what applicants' expectations are. More specifically, they have to learn what applicants think about themselves:

- their belief in their capacity to do the job, as it is and as it will become
- their expectations about what they will be asked to do
- their ambitions and hopes about what they would like to do and become
- their value priorities, and their major needs
- how open to change they are.

Organizations need to know exactly the same as individuals need to know about themselves. It's also worth noting that these are the aspects of an individual that both parties need to be aware of when discussing the individual's career development. This is an inevitable consequence of treating the selection process as a negotiating relationship; it is all part of the *continuous* negotiation of the psychological contract between employer and employee.

The organization is unlikely to be satisfied with discovering what the applicants think about themselves now and for the future. It is apt to discount the applicants' 'subjective' view of themselves in comparison to the 'objective' assessment which it believes it makes in its selection procedure. There are major problems with this attitude.

The first is this. What applicants think about themselves, and what the organization thinks about them, are not external to the relationship, but part of it. For example, applicants' degree of confidence that they can do the job affects their behaviour in the selection process and their effectiveness in a subsequent employment relationship. Initial impressions formed by an interviewer are perceived by applicants: they can see whether they are being approved of or not. This will affect their probability of successful selection and willingness to accept an offer. Assessments, in brief, are part of the selection relationship; they are not outside it.

Second, assessments are not 'objective' (the organization's) as opposed to 'subjective' (the applicant's). Rather, they are from different points of view. Different points of view offer different perspectives, and have different origins. The applicants' own point of view about themselves is based on a lifetime's evidence. They have observed themselves acting in different situations, and the consequence of these actions: the extent to which they have achieved their objectives and the reactions of others. What is more, only they have access to important features of themselves such as their intentions and aspirations. On the other hand, when comparing their capacities with those of other people, applicants are likely to exaggerate. In the selection situation, this is probably due to their desire to get the job, but it derives also from their need to have a positive view of their capacities and so preserve self-esteem. This is where the organization's point of view becomes particularly valuable, since it is in a position to compare applicants with each other.

The organization is therefore well advised to ask applicants to provide evidence for their views of themselves rather than take them at face value. Such evidence might take many forms, and organizations will need to specify what aspects of the self they want evidence about, and suggest some of the forms of evidence they consider to be appropriate.

What aspects of the self, for example, might a computer organization employing a middle manager to head a team of systems analysts be interested in?

- perceived knowledge and technical competence in systems analysis
- capacity to organize the work of the team effectively
- to liaise with other team leaders
- to deal with clients
- to understand and communicate company policy
- to develop their subordinates
- intention to remain with the organization for a reasonable period of time
- potential to learn about fifth-generation computing within 3−4 years
- capacity to fill a more senior position, and to direct their own development accordingly.

The organization will ask for applicants' self-assessment of all these aspects of the self. It will then suggest some of the forms of evidence which applicants should bring forward to support their self-assessment. Knowledge and technical com-

petence in systems analysis, for example, might be supported
by:

- a record of formal training, including the grades or
  ratings achieved (where appropriate)
- a list of positions held, the major responsibilities of each
  position, the skills acquired, and details of any projects
  for which the applicant was responsible
- records of appraisal assessments in previous positions and
  rate of promotions or salary increases, indicating how
  others evaluated this range of activities
- other activities and recognition, e.g. in professional
  associations.

Intention to stay might be supported by:

- a statement of how the position fits in with the applicant's
  overall career plan
- how long the applicant had stayed in previous positions
  relative to the industry norm and
- what would make the applicant want to leave.

Now take a 17-year-old male school leaver, wanting to
become a bank clerk.

- How confident and accurate does he think he is in routine
  numerical tasks and at using the computer?
- How capable is he of understanding the procedures of
  banking, and of learning about the variety of insurance,
  investment and mortgage facilities which banks increasingly hope to market and sell?
- How good is he at dealing with customers in a helpful
  way?
- How likely is he to be trustworthy about money and
  confidential information?
- How capable of further career development is he?
- How interested is he in banking as an occupation, and
  how committed is he to it as a career?

He might be encouraged to produce his achievement
record, which an increasing number of schools use to evidence
the variety and level of activities of pupils at school. He would

be asked to indicate those features of the record which gave pointers to each of the aspects of the self which the organization specified. Consider just the capacity to understand banking and related financial procedures. What evidence is there of the capacity to understand and acquire knowledge? Examination results will be of use, but can only be understood in the context of the life opportunities enjoyed by our applicant. Such is the increasing inequality of opportunity in the UK at present that academic achievements depend as much on the quality of education offered as on the capacities of the student.

A much more reliable and valid indication of the capacity to acquire and use job knowledge is a sound psychological test of intellectual aptitude. Such tests can give indications of the overall level of complexity of knowledge which he is capable of mastering as well as any particular aptitudes, for example in the numerical area. Their results are still affected by the life opportunities he has enjoyed, but considerably less so than his academic achievement. All young people should be given the opportunity of taking good tests of intellectual aptitude and being advised on their implications before they try to enter the job market.

Now consider another question: how interested is he in banking as an occupation, and how committed is he to it as a career? Appropriate evidence might be the results of an interest inventory, which some school leavers currently complete with the guidance of the careers advice service (where it still exists). If the organization has provided a job knowledge inventory (see page 49) in its information pack, the applicant will wish to indicate what he has learned from it, the implication being that if he now has a realistic view of the job and still applies, his interest is likely to be genuine and informed. As far as commitment to banking as a career is concerned, the bank will want to hear what other occupations he has considered. If he maintains a continuing interest in related occupations, this should tie in with the results of his interest inventory. If he sees his working life in five years' time as consistent with the bank's career structure, his aspirations may be both realistic and well informed.

Both of these examples require applicants to give rounded views of themselves in relation to the job; not just of their present capabilities, but of their potential, their interests, their aspirations. In both cases, the applicants have been asked to justify their view of themselves. Such justification is doubly important from the organization's point of view: if it has informed potential applicants clearly of what it is looking for, applicants who want the job may indicate aptitudes, potential, expectations and aspirations which match those required.

This presentation of their view of themselves and their justification for it places a heavy weight upon applicants. But as the organization has put considerable effort into informing them about itself, so they in turn may agree to making explicit a lot more than is usual about themselves. While applicants are accustomed to being asked about their prior record, they are seldom asked about their expectations and aspirations for the future. The organization may assume that applicants will describe these so as to put themselves in the best light (i.e. accord with what they think the organization wants). But this assumption is false on two counts. First, applicants may not want the job regardless of real compatibility. And, second, the organization will already have been honest about itself, so some sense of trust in the other party may have been developed.

Another reason why applicants will be willing to provide so much information is that they know why it's wanted. The organization will already have explained the reasons. Furthermore, they will welcome the fact that it is their own view of themselves which is being asked for (albeit with supporting evidence). They are likely to find this infinitely preferable to being assessed by the organization without being told:

- what is being assessed
- why it is being assessed and
- what the result of the assessment is.

Chapter 7

Contracting for the 90s: Selection

Some design features

What will the selection procedure of the 90s look like? Remember, it has to operate in a seller's market and in a changed organizational context.

First, we have to specify some general design parameters. These must be in line with the idea that the selection process is the first stage of the psychological contract between organization and employee. What are they?

- *The process must be individual, not mass.*

The essence of the psychological contract is that it is a mutual agreement between individual and organization. Thus, all procedures which treat applicants *en masse* for reasons of administrative convenience are inappropriate. Rather, the relationship needs to be individualized from the start, with each applicant being assigned to a single organizational representative throughout. Much of the initial information provided by the organization will obviously be the same for all applicants of a certain category. Nevertheless, from the beginning applicants will have their own questions which require specific answers.

● *The process must be sequenced, not haphazard.*

The selection process has to be seen as a sequence of events. In each of these events, one of the parties gives information to the other. As a consequence of this information, a decision is made – whether to carry on the relationship or quit. It is therefore important that the sequence genuinely involves exchange: if the organization receives a great deal of information in an application form, it should expect to be telling the applicant things about itself in the next event in the sequence.

● *The process must be costed, not profligate.*

Each event in the sequence is likely to prove more expensive as the sequence develops. This is because more and more detailed information is likely to be required. The initial information sent out by the organization in response to enquiries may be mass-produced; the hour spent answering questions later in the sequence is much more expensive. Similarly, it costs the applicants little to send for an application form, but it can take them a morning to complete it. Moreover, the expense is not solely in money and time, but also in self-esteem. The more detailed the information applicants give about themselves, the more they are exposing their selves, and the more hurtful rejection will be.

● *Decisions must be mutually aided, not taken in isolation.*

Suppose an applicant receives detailed information from the organization about the job. He or she has to decide whether or not to continue the relationship (for example, by sending in a completed application form). There may well be some points which need clarification, or some discrepancies between what the organization says it expects of them and what they expect to do for the organization. To take an informed decision, they need to know what the organization *really* expects, and whether it is likely to move a little closer to their own expectations. They should therefore be able to find out, by receiving easy access to someone who can tell them.

● *The sequence of events should be as short as possible.*

A good reason for reducing the number of stages in the process is that exit is most often at the very early stages of the sequence. Many applicants don't complete application forms and many are rejected as a consequence of the pre-selection sift. As a result, the majority of decisions are based on minimal information and acquaintance. Somehow the parties need to get to know each other better sooner; ways to make this happen are discussed on page 68.

● *Commitments are made at each stage, not just at the end.*
Decisions are not all-or-nothing once-for-all events which occur at a single point in time. They are gradual and incremental in nature. They are not a careful weighing up of the pros and cons of alternative courses of action. Rather, they are a matter of feeling right in a relationship. This does not mean that information has no part to play. But it is the nature of the information, and how it is given, that are crucial. An organization may admit its weak points and be trusted for being honest. It may persuade an applicant to attend an assessment centre by explaining what will happen, why they are used, what is assessed and the benefits both parties can get out of it. Applicants will feel more committed to attend if they perceive that the organization is caring enough to tell them what is going to happen and why.

This mutual trust and commitment to the other is increased as each episode occurs, and as each fulfils the other's expectations within it. At the beginning, the commitment is simply to the next episode in the procedure. However, after a while each party infers that the other will continue to behave in the same way after the employment contract is made. It is how the applicant behaves during the selection procedure which largely determines whether he or she will be selected; and it is how the organization and its representative behave which predicts to a considerable degree whether the applicant will select them. Each is basing their decision on the quality of the relationship so far.

To sum up, the design features of the selection procedure for the 90s imply the development of a relationship. This involves the sharing of information which is accurate, with the result that mutual trust develops. Care must be taken to avoid the danger which besets so many potentially promising relationships: one party breaks it off before they have found out enough about the other.

A prototype procedure

So what does the procedure of the 90s actually look like? Assume an advertisement that briefly describes the job, the number of positions available, the organization's identity and function, and an invitation to write or phone a named contact/individual for further information.

The information pack which is sent will contain:

- realistic information about the job, career and organization
- information about aptitudes, expectations, aspirations and values which are relevant to the job, now and in the future
- indications of the types of evidence which should support the applicant's self-assessment
- an invitation to some form of realistic job preview, preferably a job-sample on site (this can be coupled with an opportunity to ask questions of the contact; alternatively, the recipient may be invited to phone the contact with any queries)
- information about the rest of the selection process
- an invitation to send a self-assessment, with supporting documentation where appropriate.

Applicants will now have had a chance to:

- discover what the organization expects
- assess themselves against those expectations
- decide, as a result, whether or not to send a self-assessment.

Such a decision will depend on the degree of congruence, but not in a simple way. Applicants will keep in mind their perceptions of alternative opportunities in the labour market. They will also have a greater or lesser degree of confidence in

Recruitment in the 90s

IPM's NEW ONE DAY SEMINAR FOR SENIOR MANAGERS

A lively, participative and thought provoking event for senior managers responsible for formulating recruitment strategies, and currently anticipating their organization's recruitment needs for the 1990s. Led by Peter Herriot and designed to complement this new book, the seminar will be of special interest to those wishing to adopt a more innovative and progressive approach to recruitment. The programme will include:

- economic, political and social developments – their influence on present and future recruitment strategies

- traditional recruitment and selection techniques – how appropriate in the future?

- effective strategies and new recruitment tools for the 90s

Dates
28 June 1989
15 December 1989

Location
Chelsea Hotel
17 Sloane Street
London SW1

Cost (excluding VAT)
£194.00 IPM members
£233.00 Non-members

For full seminar programme please contact the IPM (Tel: 01-946 9100) and ask for the Course and Conference Department the organization's promise to engage in real negotiation.

A considerable proportion of those who originally responded to the advertisement are expected to self-select out at this stage, not least because the self-assessment will require considerable time, thought and effort. On the other hand, they are more likely to reciprocate if the organization itself has put time, thought and effort into the information it has already provided.

Next, the organization matches the self-assessments and supporting evidence which it has received against its own stated expectations. It is unlikely to base its decisions solely on the degree of congruence, since the quality of the supporting evidence may not confirm every aspect of the applicant's self-assessment.

On the assumption that a certain number of negotiations will fail, the organization will set up a number of final negotiation interviews somewhat in excess of the positions to be filled. Negotiations will focus on the points where expectations diverge, in an effort to reconcile the parties. These reconciliations are to result in agreements about how the applicants' career will develop within the organization. Hence the successful conclusion of a negotiation will result in an initial career-development plan which takes account of both parties' interests and to which both are committed. The psychological and employment contracts can then be synchronized and harmonized. Job satisfaction is likely to be increased and turnover decreased. Induction and socialization into the organization can be tailored to the individual and designed as part of the initial career-development plan. They can also become opportunities for personal and role development rather than techniques for enforcing conformity.

The shocking feature of the selection procedure of the 90s is that it does not involve the traditional interview, in which interviewers form impressions of and make judgements about applicants. While great efforts have been made to reduce discriminatory bias in psychological tests and assessment centres, the traditional selection interview remains riddled with opportunities to give one's prejudices full rein. It is also unreliable and invalid. The selection system of the 90s will not use the interview for selection purposes, but for negotiation after selection has been made.

The key feature of this prototype 90s selection procedure is that it puts into the hands of the applicants information presently retained by the organization. Organizations will look askance at not formally interviewing applicants before they negotiate with them. And they are likely to be unwilling to specify what they are looking for; even more, they are unlikely to give away the tools and outcomes of assessment.

What about proper assessment?

Personnel managers will be dismissing my prototype for the 90s in terms of warm fuzzies. Psychologists will be horrified at the apparent absence of reliable and valid instruments. Both would be mistaken. The procedure proposed is actually likely to result in *more* cost-beneficial outcomes, especially with regard to retention. And there is certainly a place for sound assessment tools. It is *how* they are used rather than their use *per se* which needs changing.

At present, the tools of assessment are administered by organizations. Many do not tell applicants what is being assessed, nor why they believe it necessary to assess whatever they are assessing. Most fail to inform applicants of the outcomes of the assessments, what they mean and what conclusions they are drawing from them. Applicants know they are revealing things about themselves, but they don't know what it is they are revealing. It is hardly surprising that psychological tests of aptitude and personality are markedly unpopular with applicants. Indeed, in a seller's market, it is possible that the additional benefits they bestow in selecting better people will be outweighed by the voluntary exit from the selection process of those who do not like being tested.

Information from psychological tests is essentially information about the applicant. If each party is giving the other information about themselves, then the applicant should be giving the organization assessment information. The applicants should own this information, and should release it as part of the evidence supporting their self-assessment. Accountancy firms will have described the work involved, and indicated that they believe numeracy to be an important intellectual aptitude. They may specify that they want to learn the 'O' Level Maths grade achieved, whether or not the applicant took Advanced levels or a degree which involved numerate work, and their score on the numeracy scale of one of the two or three sound and standardized tests of higher-level intellectual aptitude available in the UK.

Applicants will have already taken this test. It will have formed part of an opportunity for self-assessment provided for them. In the case of graduates, the university careers service will have provided them with the opportunity to be assessed by a careers adviser or psychologist, using tests of aptitude and personality, occupational interest inventories and other assessment devices. These can be reliable and valid forms of information about oneself.

- They can reveal the existence of a high level of an aptitude which people did not know they possessed
- They can make clear their relative strengths and weaknesses
- They can make explicit interests and preferences which they had taken for granted
- They can be of immense help in deciding which occupational direction to take.

Their *use* is the crucial factor. They are administered to individuals for the purpose of helping them learn more about themselves, and the results are explained to them. The individuals therefore *own* the information. They can retain it or reveal it as they wish. Its first function is always to inform the individual; the second may be to support a job application. Since careers services in secondary and higher education don't currently possess the resources to provide such a service, organizations should put pressure on the Government to fund them more appropriately and should be willing to help with the expense themselves. After all, they now spend large sums on psychological consultants to supply or administer tests which applicants may take on several different occasions.

The other sort of assessment device — job-sample exercises or situational interviews — can, however, be incorporated into the procedure itself. This is because these techniques perform two functions. They permit the applicant a realistic job preview, and they also allow them to assess themselves and to be assessed. Again, the outcome of the assessment should be communicated to applicants, so that they can make their own decisions about whether they will match up to the demands of the job. They can then opt out if they fall short, failing which the organization may opt out. So these techniques are doubly valuable to the applicants: they enable them to see what the work is like, and whether they are interested in doing it; they also permit them to see how good at it they are likely to be.

So the shape of the selection procedure of the 90s matches its design principles. These in turn are dictated by the shortfall of human resources and the rise in demand for them. To quote another person in another place, there is no alternative. To a large extent, we can't buy them and we can't make them. We can't select them, since they are also selecting us. All we can do is contract with them. The race is on to design and establish user-friendly selection systems.

Chapter 8

Contracting for the 90s: Retention

Flexibility in career management

From the organization's point of view, the new circumstances of the 90s mean that the retention of human resources is crucial. There will be less of them around; they will be more expensive to replace; and they will have had much more spent on their development. Given that early broad-based development *and* specialized technical training will be necessary for the managers of the 90s, organizations won't reap the benefits until quite a few years of employment have elapsed.

It's hard not to feel sympathy for them. The labour market has see-sawed alarmingly in the 60s, 70s, and 80s. A seller's market in the 60s and 70s became a buyer's one in the early 80s. Effective organizations got around to changing human-resource strategies to cope. They realized the cost-benefit advantages of selecting carefully from a considerable excess of applicants over vacancies, and they developed selection, appraisal and promotion methods accordingly. Suddenly they are faced with another pendulum swing, back to the seller's market of the 90s. They have to cope with the implied changes in human-resource policies and practices which have been redesigned in consequence.

But the pendulum of resource availability isn't the only disturbance in their environment. There are fashions in human-resource management which resemble nothing as much as the permissive versus authoritarian trends in bringing up children. Unfortunately for organizations, it's not just one pendulum that's swinging but several simultaneously. Here are some of them:

● *Specialists or generalists?*
  Given the increasingly technological nature of today's businesses, we need more highly trained professionals. But given the rapidly changing nature of our markets, we need versatile people who can expand a particularly booming function (marketing? design?). And given the strategic nature of senior management, we must also have people with a broad overview of the organization.

● *Centralization or decentralization?*
  Are organizational human-resource policy and executive decisions best located at headquarters, where individual careers can be planned to fit in with organizational requirements, or should local line managers have the responsibility for the careers and development of their subordinates? If people such as scientists and engineers are a precious and rare resource, should their careers not be a matter for careful central control? Yet if control *is* centralized, will they be suitable and useful on the ground?

● *Home-grown or bought-in?*
  Should we develop our own talent or should we buy in appropriately qualified people when necessary? Native talent has absorbed the company culture and can be relied on, but it has to be developed in the round if it is to be able to fill new positions. Bought-in people bring new ideas from other organizations, and can be carefully tailored to a particular position; but their recruitment can be very difficult and expensive, sometimes costing as much as two years of the employee's financial benefits or 'added value' to the organization.

● *Steep or flat structures?*
Multiple levels in the hierarchy result in either excessively lengthy or contentiously leapfrogging career paths; few levels means that the move to the next level is pretty abrupt.

● *Fast-stream and professional or generalist career paths?*
Specialized and high-flying cohorts can be carefully groomed; but their size is constant as they pass through the organization, so allowing little flexibility to cope with changes in the numbers required. What's more, they demotivate the others. General career paths don't have these disadvantages; but are they capable of throwing up the necessary specialists and top management?

● *Individual development or specific training?*
Individuals can be encouraged to develop their own knowledge and skills, or the organization can decide what their training needs are. In the former case, organizations often state their commitment to a policy of individual development but fail to provide the opportunity. In the latter, the orientation is often towards remedying an unmet skill requirement in the present situation rather than preparing for the future.

All these pendula have been swinging vigorously in the last decade. Some of them, as Wendy Hirsh at the Institute of Manpower Studies has noted, have been swinging in contradictory directions. An emphasis on greater professionalization and more experts in organizations has coincided with a decentralization of the personnel function; the consequence has been a lack of planning of specialist careers. Sometimes, these contradictory swings even occur simultaneously: organizations have been known to groom a fast stream for succession to top management, then chicken out and buy in.

The 90s will see the end of these fashionable swings in human-resource policy. They will themselves be out of fashion. For all of the either/ors we have listed will have to become both/ands:

● There won't be specialists or generalists. The managers will all be specialists, in the sense that they will all have started out with some technical skill. They will all be generalists as well, though. For each of them will have acquired, at the very least, one other technical competence: complete understanding of the uses of information technology.

- Centralization or decentralization of career planning won't be a workable distinction either. Information about available opportunities and positions anywhere in the organization will be available and addressable by information technology to all employees.

- Organizations will have to grow their own *and* buy in people if they are to be flexible enough. But it is the home-grown core who will have the scarce skills and specific knowledge the organization needs. Peripheral workers can be easily hired if their skills are not in short supply.

- Hierarchies, whether flat or steep, will be edifices of the past – different models of antique pyramid. Flexible organizations need the old up-or-out slogan like they need a take-over bid. Instead, they will offer multiple career paths where progression and promotion are not synonymous.

- This proliferation of different sequences of positions means that rigid cohorts of fast-streamers and general-management trainees who leap up and sideways at the same time will be creatures of the past.

- It also means that each individual's development needs will be different, and therefore that the organization will have to plan for the future with each of them. Long-term potential, not short-term performance, will be the focus of mutual attention.

All of these developments will be forced upon organizations by the realities of the 90s. Functional requirements will change rapidly, as marketing, design, and research and development gain greater prominence. Entirely new skills and new jobs will emerge, while a continuing relentless emphasis on short-term financial results will militate against the longer view. Flexibility in the use of human resources will be the key to survival in the search for the competitive edge.

Life careers and work careers

But it is not just in response to markets for goods and services that organizations need to be flexible. They must also respond to the labour market. In a seller's market, key employees will have expectations for their careers which will have to be met. Otherwise they will take themselves off elsewhere. What are these expectations likely to be? How is the organization going to be flexible enough to meet them? And how is this flexibility which is needed in order to retain staff to be made compatible with the flexibility required to match market needs? Both organizations and employees want less predictability, less uniformity, in careers, although for different reasons. But will they be pulling in the same or opposite directions?

One of the reasons organizations find it hard to retain valued employees is that they make faulty assumptions about what staff expect. They mostly believe that employees want a transactional form of contract − external rewards such as pay, perks and status are exchanged for good performance and high effort. But that may not be the sort of contract employees always have in mind. They may want a much more relational sort of psychological contract. In return for long-term loyalty and readiness to develop themselves, they may want security of employment and/or some fit between their work career and their life career.

Up until now organizations have almost totally failed to pay attention to the life careers of their employees. They can only cope with organizational reality − the realities of daily life are beyond them. They have been able to continue in this willful ignorance only because of the 'good little woman at home' syndrome. Organizations have happily assumed that domestic and family arrangements are managed elsewhere and by someone else. They can assume so no longer. First, single-parent families are increasingly common; second, in order to afford housing in the South-East, both partners in a relationship *have to* work (quite apart from all questions of personal satisfaction). So what are the life commitments that people take on?

Commitments to a partner, to a mortgage, to children, to their education, to the community, to ageing parents, all follow each other at what feels like breakneck speed. Then, with similar suddenness, twenty years later, children leave and parents die. Consider more closely commitments to children: adapting to the birth of the first; coping with several before they attend school; soothing the multiple pimples and perils of adolescence; gentle pushing from the nest.

Now these are stereotypic life careers, the supposed norm to which there are ever more exceptions. But for people who do have this typical life career, how does the typical organizational career mesh in with it? The answer is that it doesn't merely fail to mesh — it clashes horribly. The move to middle management in the late 20s and early 30s coincides with the onset of several of life's major commitments. The typical organizational requirement for middle-management mobility in the late 30s and early 40s coincides with the commitment to education and community. For single parents (most of whom are women), the commitments are all-consuming. If organizations cannot even cope with the supposedly typical family pattern, how can they hope to manage some of the more unusual varieties?

Career contracts

There are alternatives. Individuals' career paths can be tailored to both the organization's and their own needs. The organization needs long-term loyalty and employees willing to develop in the directions indicated by its human-resource strategy. Individuals want periods when they can reconcile their work and life commitments. Perhaps the key to sensible planning is to look at when new commitments start. It is no good an employee being moved into a new development position at the same point in time as they are about to produce their first offspring. The combination of demands from different sources is what puts extra stress on individuals and their relationships.

In order to coordinate work and life careers, organizations have to plan their human-resource moves in advance. Only if they are aware in advance of the approaching need to increase resources in certain functional areas can such planning take place. Human-resource policies require strategic planning in the light of knowledge of the corporate strategy and the labour market. Never again can the human-resource function be treated as an administrative necessity, staffed by those with no particular skills or training.

Let's look at mobility as a specific instance of a potential clash between work and life commitments. Organization A, a large computer company, has realized that to retain its competitive edge it needs to increase its marketing function and its advisory services to clients. It therefore needs to develop some of its technical people, especially systems designers, to undertake these new roles. It will also require them to move, since while research, design and development are centrally located, the marketing and consultancy functions are regional. The organization, therefore:

- allocated the mobility issue to a senior manager in the human-resource staff
- discovered what the mobility patterns had been for the target groups of employees in the previous five years
- worked out the approximate number of transfers required, the nature and length of the necessary conversion training, and a flexible time scale for the whole operation
- informed the target employees of all the above, as well as giving a detailed account of the nature of the marketing and consultancy work and career prospects within them
- invited declarations of initial interest, without commitment at this stage
- conducted one-to-one interviews with all those declaring an interest. These were intended both to inform and to negotiate. The interviewer was empowered to make individual agreements, within certain parameters of cost and time

- discovered what non-financial assistance employees needed, and provided it where possible
- discovered what incentives the employee wanted and negotiated on the basis of those, rather than automatically on the basis of promotion, perks and pay. Expectations became modified, and turned into mutually accepted obligations.

John Atkinson of the Institute of Manpower Studies found in 1987 that four out of ten managers and professionals had relocated in the past 10 years. One third of his sample had rejected a job offer because it involved relocation. Firms thought that house prices were the main obstacle, whereas in fact employees were much more concerned with quality-of-life issues: disruption to social and family networks; problems with house purchase; and the attractiveness of the area.

Contracting or culture control?

More generally, this organization's response to its relocation needs demonstrates how human-resource systems can be geared to policies. What it did was to make clear its own expectations, discover what its employees' expectations were, and negotiate on that basis. If psychological contracting of this nature is to form the basis of human-resource policy, how can practices be redesigned accordingly? We have already discussed in detail how recruitment and selection will have to change. What about other systems?

All human-resource systems will have to be designed so as to facilitate negotiation and ensure that obligations are met. This means that:

- Both parties will have to make clear their expectations, at regular intervals
- They will have to negotiate regularly and arrive at mutually acceptable contracts
- They will have to check up to see that contracts are being kept

- Organizations will have to realize that individual employees differ in terms of their motivations, and in terms of their current life commitments
- Employees will have to understand the organization's need for flexibility in allocating its human resources.

Given these design features, appraisals, job redesign, performance reviews, reward systems, training and development all become opportunities for renegotiating and checking up on psychological contracts. Personal development is not a reward for good individual performance, but is mutually beneficial to organization and employee alike.

Currently, many organizations are moving in diametrically the opposite direction, away from real psychological contracting. They are seeking to engineer commitment to the organization by manipulating its culture. Control over employees is increased by these indirect and implicit means.

Culture consists of artefacts, values and assumptions about reality, according to Ed Schein. Hence an organization's culture is signalled by its artefacts. What does its annual appraisal form look like? How long is it, and does it permit the employees to appraise themselves? What are the organizational myths − stories of past triumphs and their causes? Does it rely on slogans like 'The customer is always right'? All of these artefacts express values and assumptions. Change the artefacts, runs the argument, and you set the scene for changing the values. At the very least, you have to change the artefacts accordingly if you succeed in changing the values by other means.

Value priorities can be changed, too. In the UK, the traditional high value attached to equitable treatment of employees in the public sector has been downgraded relative to the value attached to the efficient use of resources. In universities, the high value associated with the advancement of scientific knowledge has been largely replaced by immediate commercial relevance. Many consultants succeed in turning around private-sector companies by making the achievement of profitability the single most valued outcome.

Underlying artefacts and values are basic beliefs − often

beliefs about human nature. Examples of such beliefs might be the idea that everyone is motivated by salary and promotion; that increased effort leads to improved performance; that people live to work rather than work to live; that personal qualities are responsible for individual performance.

Now all of these artefacts, values and beliefs are the targets of the organizational culture engineers. They seek to induce organizational commitment by engineering an overlap between the organization's and employees' expectations. If both parties believe that all employees may reasonably be expected to agree to relocation on request, then the need for negotiation is removed. If employees and organizations both believe that the value of all work can be quantified financially, then there will be no disagreement about methods of performance evaluation.

Yet all such attempts at engineering cultural changes are trying to induce unitary organizational control instead of encouraging diverse individual interests. To deny individual interests is to deny the importance of all relationships other than that between the individual and the organization. Such a denial is completely contrary both to reality and to the value systems of most of the graduates of the 90s. Those organizations which insist on complete conformity and devotion to a very strong corporate culture retain only those who have a strong need to belong, and who achieve their identity through belonging. Loyalty, hard work and obedience cannot compensate for the ability to perceive problems and solve them innovatively. Really far-sighted organizations nurture talented people, give them space, and let them loose in it.

Let's conclude our discussion of retention by looking at the particular set of employees whom it will be the most important to retain in the 90s. I am referring to the scarcest resources of all: natural scientists, engineers, and computer scientists. There is one feature which distinguishes these professionals – their professional identity. Many of them owe their allegiance to and get their kudos from professional colleagues, *wherever they are employed*. The American sociologist, Gouldner, called them 'cosmopolitans': people whose horizons are far wider than their own organization. They go to conferences, hold office in professional associations, travel abroad to meet colleagues and so on. Their interest and motivation is in doing their specialist job well, and in becoming known and recognized for being at the sharp end, the cutting edge of scientific or technological innovation.

Now Gouldner contrasted 'cosmopolitans' with 'locals' – people who gain their identity from their organizational membership and loyalty. Organizations tend to make the same distinction; and in the headlong pursuit of organizational commitment, they put it around that the two orientations are incompatible. All employees must be locals. Nothing is less likely to increase the organizational commitment of professionals. The wise organization helps professionals enhance their professional identity and supports their cosmopolitan orientation. After all, if that's one of their prime expectations from working life, the organization which meets it retains them.

We can see what happens when organizations don't pay any attention to professional aspirations in the UK at the moment. In the public sector, professionals are leaving in droves: nurses, teachers, lecturers, scientists all say they cannot do their jobs to their professional satisfaction. The thrust for public sector efficiency and managerial control has turned away the people who do the basic work.

In fact, of course, organizations benefit no end from catering to their professionals' cosmopolitan identity. The professionals learn about what's going on elsewhere from colleagues in other organizations: the only way to stay at the cutting edge is to keep up with the field. Collaboration between organizationally based and academic scientists has resulted in the discovery and exploitation of several of the most profitable and worthwhile drug treatments and information technologies. By way of further evidence, some of the early research on biographical data showed that R and D scientists with professional ties took out more patents than those who played little or no part in their professional associations.

So if organizations want to retain professionals in the 90s they will:

- positively encourage professional membership and qualifications
- encourage evaluation by outside peers
- permit the maximum degree of autonomy consistent with organizational policy
- appoint professionals as managers of other professionals
- ensure that these managers' prime objective is the effectiveness of their professional work, rather than efficiency.

It is only when professionals are encouraged to work to their own high standards and to the satisfaction of their peers that they will also come to see their professional aspirations as serving the organization's objectives.

Some revealing figures are given in Table 6 (see Appendix). While there is obviously a wide variation in retention rates between sectors, it is noteworthy that engineers (for example) have a very high turn-over rate. This no doubt reflects employer attitudes as well as the different job markets.

Chapter 9
Objections and Prospects

'What these ivory tower merchants don't realize is that it's a competitive world. In the early 80s we were competing for the best. Now we're competing just for our fair share. Do you think we're going to let up and allow the competition to get in there ahead of us? Anyway, you're asking me to do a whole lot more in the recruitment line and my budget's not increased in real terms in the last 10 years. And what's all this about telling the punters how we're going to select them? That's a sure-fire recipe for disaster. They'll be put off for good when we tell them what we're going to do to them or else they'll just try to pull the wool over our eyes. And our competitors will find out all about our methods and copy them; we spend a lot of money developing them − why should they get them for free?'

Here are some questions in reply!

- What are you competing for?
- Are you competing for applications?
- Are you competing for people who will accept your job offer?
- Are you competing for people *who will stay for at least three years*?

Most organizations, especially in the graduate recruitment market, compete for applications. They spend large amounts of money on promotional literature and attract as many as 50 applications for each position they have to offer. They then reduce these applications down to 2 or 3 per position by two almost random procedures – the pre-selection sift and the milk-round interview – incurring considerable costs as they do so. The bottom line for the recruitment function is whether it succeeds in filling the positions or not. But the number of applications attracted is also a popular index of success.

Have they ever looked at the other sets of figures? How many of those who were invited to interview actually turned up? How many invited to second interview turned up? How many accepted their job offer? How many, having accepted, still failed to start work with them? And how many of those they would have liked to retain left within 2 or 3 years?

It is really worthwhile disentangling the two sets of choices – those of the organization and those of the applicant – looking at them separately and relating them to costs. The proportion of rejections by the organization to rejections by the applicant at each stage is an important index here. And even if at the earlier stages the organization is rejecting proportionately more applicants than vice versa, its selectivity isn't effective if those it ultimately offers jobs to don't accept, don't turn up or don't stay.

If the bottom line becomes that of retaining the people the organization wishes to retain for longer than 2 or 3 years, then the emphasis should be on contracting rather than selecting. In other words, we would expect more self-selecting out at early stages, hence less applications in the first place, and less subsequent rejection of each other by both parties. Costs will probably remain about the same: the costs of glossy promotions and many interviews will be replaced by those of full information and individual attention. But cost effectiveness should increase, since retention of staff for over 2–3 years should improve and the costs of buying in to replace early leavers are avoided. Commitment to the organization consequent upon contracting means that employees don't merely use the organization to obtain professional qualification or training.

'What sort of people do you think applicants are? And, for that matter, how well can you spot people who hype themselves?'

Your second objection to my proposals for recruitment and retention was that applicants would seek to pull the wool over recruiters' eyes if they were told the procedures that would be used in the recruitment process. Perhaps Freud rides again, and recruiters are happily projecting onto others what they think they themselves would do in their situation! More seriously, Clive Fletcher of Goldsmiths College has produced evidence suggesting that graduates at least are a lot less Machiavellian in the employment interview than we give them 'credit' for. And Tony Keenan of Heriot Watt found that Machiavellianism doesn't help them anyway; indeed, the Machiavellians did slightly worse than the straightforward applicants.

The procedure I have proposed actually requires quite a lot from those who do decide to apply, after having found out about the organization and its recruitment procedure. It asks them for information about themselves which can in principle be verified. Details of previous experience and achievements and records of psychological assessments are much less likely to be consciously distorted than self-presentations at interview. Research on the veracity of application forms indicates that the more verifiable the information asked for, the less likely applicants are to falsify it.

But there is another reason why the self-descriptions of applicants will probably be honest. The organization will have already established a relationship of trust by being honest about itself in its initial information. Of course, the applicant is unlikely to know for sure on the basis of evidence how honest it is. But he or she is likely to infer honesty if the picture presented isn't all wine and roses.

What if other organizations find out about your selection procedures? It's not the end of the world. There is no magic selection device which will solve all your problems, nor will there ever be. What there is is a set of more or less reliable and valid selection tools which have to be put together into a selection procedure. How the procedure is designed is the crucial factor, and this depends on the organization and its objectives. If the aim is to attract and retain long-term core employees, the overall design and the individual tools used will be different from those used when there is an avowed need for short-term labour. If the target employees are computer scientists, the procedure will differ from that required for less scarce personnel managers. Anyway, most of the newer and more fashionable tools have to be developed within house. Assessment centre exercises are best based on job samples; situational interviews likewise depend on a careful job analysis.

As for putting off potential applicants by telling them how you're going to select them, it all depends what you're going to ask them to do, what they are going to get out of it, and how you tell them. Many applicants, especially graduates, are very anxious to know what the work is like and whether they are any good at it. All types of job sample, whether in exercise or question form, are welcome, more particularly if feedback about performance is given. Even psychological tests of aptitude may perhaps be acceptable, provided it is explained why they are being used. For example, while a mathematics graduate may rightly feel insulted to be given a test of numerical aptitude, an arts graduate who is trying for a job with a large numeracy requirement might well see the point. Knowledge of the results will be especially useful to such an applicant, since it will help her to decide whether or not to apply for similar jobs in the future.

'Well, maybe I'll think about redesigning the selection procedure. But all this continuous contracting business is out of the question. We've got to be able to transfer people willy-nilly when we need to: the situation's changing so fast that we've got to keep maximum flexibility. As for employing retired people or parents part-time, that's just not on. We'd have to redesign jobs, redesign employment contracts, redesign the whole personnel system ...'

The best way to reply to this is by asking some more questions! For example, how flexible are you now? Perhaps the flexibility you mention is simply transfer between a few well-trodden career paths. Have you actually analysed the career paths of your middle and senior managers? How many distinct paths are there? Why did they travel these paths rather than the many other possible but unused paths? Historical accident? The need for broad experience? The belief that experience in Job X is necessary for Job Y?

Now try an exercise: draw the other possible career paths. Why haven't they been trodden up till now? Is it because of certain taken-for-granted assumptions? Is it really true, for example, that

- every next job must be upwards?
- all jobs are full-time?
- movement has to be from more specialized to more general management?
- the best available person should be allocated to each vacant job?
- perceived equity is a guiding criterion?
- different businesses/departments in the organization should try to hang on to their best people?

How many of these assumptions are really justified? On what sort of evidence are they based? What sort of organizational politics do they imply? Above all, to what extent are they based on real psychological contracting? Many of these assumptions actually imply that the organization's interests, systems and internal politics are paramount. They thus imply a false belief about what its real interests are. The most basic interest is to *survive*, and if it cannot retain its core employees it won't survive. Employees will leave if their expectations aren't being considered – if equity, politics and short-term expediency are the real criteria.

Another question concerns the implementation of career policies. How far are they constrained by your existing personnel systems and procedures?

For example, if appraisal is concerned both with reward for performance and with future development, and if reward for performance is based on some quantified measure of output, then inevitably development and performance will be confounded. Career development will be discussed on the basis of measured current performance. This can mean that a regular full-time job becomes necessary for career development, since it is only when output can be compared that differential rewards for the same jobs can be given.

To take another example, if the organization has a management training centre with an annual menu of residential courses, then only those who can work full-time are likely to be able to attend them. The same things that prevent part-timers from working full-time are going to prevent them from attending residential training courses.

Again, most of the parents working part-time are likely to be women. If there is no explicit and effective equal-opportunities policy, these employees are likely to be doubly handicapped in their career development. In other words, the practices and systems should match the human-resource policy, rather than the tail wagging the dog.

'All of this is all very well, but I've got a cat in hell's chance of getting it through. Personnel in my organization has about as much power as my grandma's motor mower.'

David Guest of the London School of Economics has speculated about why you are not alone in your feeling of powerlessness. He asks whether dressing up Personnel in the terminology of Human Resource Management is anything more than a gimmick to try and enhance your image. The use of new labels is obviously an attempt to change the culture. Artefacts such as names and documents and practices are generated by the culture and thus become symbols of it. Hence if you change the artefacts, runs the somewhat cynical message, you may succeed in having an impact in the opposite direction. In this case, the impact aimed for, of course, is a very profound culture change: personnel should become a policy-making rather than an administrative function. HRM would then begin to have a significant influence on corporate planning, since the implications for human-resource policy would have to be considered by corporate planners.

It's not cultural engineering which will bring this about, though; it's events in the outside world. For all sorts of reasons, the need for profitability in the short term has dominated British organizations in the last decade. In 1987 and 1988, however, things have changed. The Investment in British industry has increased apace, so that by the Summer of 1988 it has reached the level at which it stood in 1979. The main engine for this surge in longer-term financial support has probably been a market one: consumer demand has increased in leaps and bounds, so that domestic production has fallen behind imported goods in satisfying it. Organizations cannot design and make new products and services fast enough, nor open or refurbish production facilities. Much of manufacturing industry laid waste in 1979, 1980 and 1981 is coming to life again.

Now it is instructive to note how this increase in research and development investment, and indeed in long-term capital investment in general, came about. It was not so much planned in advance as a reaction to a booming and perhaps overheating economy. Investors are still hedging their bets, because the strength may be taken out of domestic demand by a Chancellor determined to avoid a major balance of payments problem and to keep inflation down to a reasonable level. Thus the environmental stimulus to which investors have reacted may be only a temporary one, and is certainly subject to political pressures and governmental control.

The parallel with the 1990s is instructive. As far as organizations are concerned, the environmental factor which will dominate the decade is not a financial one, it is a people one. Just as it took a consumer boom to make investors react in the late 1980s, so it will take an unprecedented shortage of human resources to make organizations react in the 90s. But there's a major difference. The consumer boom was predicted by far-sighted and hard-nosed economists, although their track record was not so perfect as to persuade even harder-nosed investors until after the event. The shortage in human resources, on the other hand, is for absolute certain.

There is, therefore, absolutely no reason why organizations should not behave proactively. But the change implied is a profound one. Just as the level of capital investment and consumer demand are changing corporate strategies in the late 80s, so the shortage of human resources will change them in the 90s. It is not a matter of corporate policy being reflected in human-resource policy. Rather, it is a human-resource problem affecting corporate policy. What will these effects be?

When we look again at the manpower projections outlined in Chapter 1, we can see where the major shortfalls will be. There will be *far* (perhaps 25 per cent) too few engineers, scientists, computer people and designers. There will probably be enough people with business and administration qualifications, since applications for these courses have increased by 13 per cent over the period 1985 to 1987. Thus it is the research, design, development and manufacture or provision of goods and services which are at risk. The internal control and maintenance of organizations is likely to be better catered for, and so are their marketing and sales. There will be lots of middle managers keeping people in order on the basis of their 'general management skills'. There will be lots more busily polishing images, either as employees or consultants. How interesting that we call such occupations 'creative'; real creativity means creating things that people want or need, not creating the want itself.

But back to the 90s. If the capacity for developing new products and services is limited by lack of people, fewer eggs will have to be put into the organizational basket. The response to the 80s consumer boom of diversifying into more product ranges will have to give way to concentration on fewer. And each line will have to be more carefully researched and developed, since the risks it carries are proportionately greater. The shortage of scientists and engineers, therefore, will have a double effect: it will mean a decrease in the number of products overall, and an increase in the research and development costs of each product which is put on the market.

Corporate strategy, as a result, will be directed far more than at present towards basic decisions regarding the products and services which organizations provide. Senior management will have to be highly selective in its choices. As it does so, it becomes yet more dependent on retaining the specialists needed for the few product lines upon which it has concentrated. One way of retaining them is to adopt the human-resource strategy of psychological contracting advocated in this book. Another is to ensure that senior management represents their point of view.

This can only happen credibly if a good proportion of senior management consists of people who have actually researched, designed or produced the product. The domination of senior management in the UK by finance people will have to be redressed. It is certainly not paralleled among our Continental rivals, where scientists and engineers are later developed into senior managers and board members as a matter of course. Our current preoccupation with the mass development of the skills and knowledge of 'general management' in those still wet behind the ears will have to give way to the retention and development of specialists. Their earlier development will be in terms of the management of research and development, production or whatever; later, they will tackle strategic planning and policy when they move over into a senior management position.

But the people who design and make the core product of the organization are not the only ones due for promotion. Just as the key task of the 80s for many organizations was to achieve survival by profitability, so the key task of the 90s is to achieve it by producing a quality product. Hence accountants and financial people will give way not just to engineers and scientists, but to human-resource specialists as well. For the production of quality products is utterly dependent upon the attraction, retention and development of specialists, and human-resource practitioners claim to be good at these tasks.

So the human resources professional of the 90s can become a key figure. He or she can:

- investigate the nature of the human-resources shortfall in terms of his or her own organization
- draw out its implications for corporate policy, with respect to the choice and development of products and services
- ensure that these implications are taken into account not

only in corporate policy but also in human-resource policy
- direct this policy towards the attraction, retention and long-term development of specialists
- redesign all human-resource systems and practices in the light of these policy requirements
- redesign selection procedures along the lines of the psychological contract, i.e. negotiate and contract so as to meet as many of the expectations of both organization and individual as possible.

If organizations don't use their human-resource profes-sionals to help them change well in advance of the 90s shortfall, the consequences could be dire. Already, many of those UK organizations which are subsidiaries of multi-national companies have surrendered their specialist functions. We can see it happening in the automobile, aviation and electronic industries, and chemicals, pharma-ceuticals and information technology are all threatened. The national prospect of acting simply as a source of labour to make goods or provide services researched and designed elsewhere is not a happy one.

Along with these attempts to cope with the shortfall of the 90s, however, should go longer-term thinking about why the shortfall occurred, and how to prevent it recurring in the 21st century. Ultimately, these are questions about political and social values and the institutions which embody them. We have to create educational institutions and organizations which encourage people to perceive new possibilities, and to collaborate with others in bringing them about. These are social and corporate moral imperatives, the warp and woof of national life. As a result, a high national value placed upon education – the lifelong development of intellectual, social and moral potential – is the best way to prevent the debacle of the 90s from ever occurring again.

References

C. Argyris, *Integrating the Individual and the Organization.* New York: Wiley, 1964.

J. Atkinson, *Re-locating Managers and Professional Staff.* Brighton: Institute of Manpower Studies, 1987.

R. E. Boyatzis, *The Competent Manager: A Model for Effective Performance.* New York: Wiley, 1982.

J. Constable and R. McCormick, *The Making of British Managers.* London: BIM/CBI, 1987.

C. Fletcher, 'Candidates' belief and self-presentation strategies in selection interviews'. *Personnel Review,* 10 (1981), 14–17.

A. W. Goulder, 'Cosmopolitans and locals: towards an analysis of latent social roles'. *Administrative Science Quarterly,* 2 (1957), 282-92.

C. Handy, *The Making of Managers.* London: MSC/NEDC/BIM, 1987.

W. Hirsh and S. Bevan, *What makes a Manager? In search of a language for management skills.* Brighton: Institute of Manpower Studies, 1988.

W. Hirsh. *Career Management in the Organization.* Brighton: Institute of Manpower Studies, 1984.

A. Keenan, *Machiavellianism and interpersonal influence in the selection interview.* Unpublished mss. Edinburgh: Heriot-Watt University, 1980.

H. Mintzberg, *The Nature of Managerial Work.* New Jersey: Prentice-Hall, (2nd edn.) 1980.

E. H. Schein, *Career Dynamics.* Reading, Mass.: Addison-Wesley, 1978.

H. A. Simon, *The New Science of Management Decisions.* New York: Harper & Row, 1960.

A. Toffler, *The Third Wave.* New York: Morrow, 1980.

Further Reading

1. Work in the Future
   C. Handy, *The Future of Work*. Oxford: Blackwell, 1984.
2. Personnel Selection (in rough order of difficulty)
   C. Lewis, *Employee Selection*. London: Hutchinson, 1985.
   M. Smith and I.T. Robertson, *Systematic Staff Selection*.
   London: Macmillan, 1986.
   P. Herriot (ed.), *Handbook of Assessment In Organisations*
   (in press) Chichester: Wiley, 1989.
   P. Herriot, *Down from the Ivory Tower: Graduates and their
   Jobs*. Chichester: Wiley, 1984.
3. Appraisal and Career Development
   C. Fletcher and R. Williams, *Performance Appraisal and
   Career Development*. London: Hutchinson, 1986.
4. Current Practice in the UK
   I.T. Robertson and P.J. Makin, 'Management selection in
   Britain: A survey and critique'. *Journal of Occupational
   Psychology*, 59 (1986), 45–57.
   W. Hirsh and S. Bevan, *What makes a Manager? In search of
   a language for management skills*. Brighton: Institute of
   Manpower Studies, 1988.
5. The reliability, validity, utility and fairness of various selection
   methods.
   R.R. Reilly and G.T. Chao, 'Validity and fairness of some
   alternative employee selection procedures'. *Personnel
   Psychology*, 35 (1982), 1–62.
   J.E. Hunter and R.F. Hunter, 'Validity and utility of
   alternative predictors of job performance'. *Psychological
   Bulletin*, 96 (1984), 72–98.

N. Schmitt, R.Z. Gooding, R.A. Noe and M. Kirsch, 'Meta analysis of validity studies published between 1964 and 1982'. *Personnel Psychology*, 37 (1984), 407–22.
6. Psychological Tests
   A. Anastasi, *Psychological Testing* (5th ed.). New York: MacMillan, 1982.
7. Interviews
   P. Herriot, 'The Selection Interview', in P.B. Warr (ed.) *Psychology At Work* (3rd ed.). Harmondsworth: Penguin, 1987.
8. Assessment Centres
   G.C. Thornton and W.C. Byham, *Assessment Centres and Managerial Performance*. New York: Academic Press, 1982.
9. Realistic Job Previews
   S.L. Premack and J.P. Wanous, 'A meta-analysis of realistic job preview experiments'. *Journal of Applied Psychology*, 70 (1985), 706–19.

Appendix

Table 1

Number of students in higher education: past and future
(thousands)

Year:	1985	1990	1996	2000
Total:	693	726	691	723

Source: Government White Paper, 'Higher Education — Meeting the Challenge', Command 114, 1987.

Table 2

**Government expenditure on universities, total and per student,
1978–90**

Year	Total expenditure (in £ million)	Per student (£)	New undergraduate entrants (thousands)
1978–9	1,120	4,352	73.0
1979–80	1,156	4,387	74.7
1980–81	1,267	4,672	76.4
1981–2	1,211	4,380	74.0
1982–3	1,401	5,095	71.6
1983–4	1,397	5,147	69.2
1984–5	1,371	5,096	70.5
1985–6	1,325	4,915	70.3
1986–7	1,320	4,855	70.7
*1987–8	1,394	5,067	72.0
*1988–9	1,442	5,145	73.6
*1989–90	1,441	5,059	75.7
*1990–91	1,424	4,942	74.2

*Estimated figures only

'Expenditure' refers to the University Grants Committee Recurrent Grant
to Universities; all figures are given at constant 1986–7 prices.

Source: Hansard, 135, 1453 and 1454.

Table 3

Percentage of organizations (n = 179) reporting difficulties in recruiting graduates in particular disciplines, June 1988

Discipline	Industrial Organizations (n = 111)	Non-industrial Organizations (n = 68)	All (n = 179)
Electronics and electrical engineering	41	19	33
Computer Studies	26	22	25
Engineering/technology	50	15	36
Science	28	6	20
Business/management studies	6	16	10
Accountancy	19	16	18
Social Studies	1	0	1
Arts	2	2	2
Other disciplines	14	21	17
All disciplines	8	37	19

Source: H. Connor, and S. Canham, *Graduate Salary and Vacancy Survey,* June 1988 update, Brighton, Institute of Manpower Studies.

Table 4

Frequency of individual assessment words in 88 assessment documents derived from 41 UK organizations

Oral communication	53
Leadership	46
Judgement	36
Initiative	34
Organizing	32
Communication	29
Motivation	28
Analytical skills	25
Professional/technical skills	22
Planning	22
Innovation	22
Appearance	22
Interpersonal skills	22
Experience	20
Numeracy	20
Maturity	20

Source: W. Hirsh, and S. Bevan, *What Makes a Manager?* Brighton, Institute of Manpower Studies, 1988.

Table 5

Table 5: Use of different management-selection methods in 108 UK organizations

	Interview	References	Cognitive tests	Personality tests	Biodata	Assessment centres
Never used (% of organizations)	1	4	71	64	94	79
Always used (% of organizations)	81	67	5	4	2	0

Adapted from I.T. Robertson and P.J. Makin, 'Management selection in Britain: A survey and critique', *Journal of Occupational Psychology*, 59 (1986), pp 45–57.

Table 6

Percentage graduate retention in different sectors

Sector	Year of Recruitment				
	1980	1981	1982	1983	1984
Civil engineering, architecture, building	61	75	82	91	100
Oil, mining, extractive	49	62	69	83	98
Chemical and allied	74	75	76	77	97
Engineering and allied	40	58	60	78	88
Food, drink and tobacco	63	67	69	75	95
Other manufacturing	54	67	78	81	97
Public utilities	67	70	81	89	99
Financial services	61	64	77	88	97
Transport and communications	62	73	75	87	98
Other professions, commerce, services	48	63	67	82	99
All sectors	58	66	72	84	94

This survey was conducted in Spring 1985 and gives figures for the percentage of graduates recruited at the end of the five previous academic years who were still working for the same firm at that time.

Source: D.J. Parsons, *Graduate Recruitment and Retention,* Brighton, Institute of Manpower Studies, 1985.

Index